Welfare and the Ageing Experience

A multidisciplinary analysis

Edited by
BILL BYTHEWAY
JULIA JOHNSON
For the British Society of Gerontology

Avebury

Aldershot · Brookfield USA · Hong Kong · Singapore · Sydney

© British Society of Gerontology 1990

Published by
Avebury
Gower Publishing Company Limited
Gower House
Croft Road
Aldershot
Hants GU11 3HR
England

Gower Publishing Company
Old Post Road
Brookfield
Vermont 05036
USA

Camera-ready copy prepared using MS-Windows, Ami Professional and Glyphix fonts.

British Library Catloguing in Publication Data
Welfare and the ageing experience : a multidisciplinary
    analysis.
    1. Welfare services for old persons
    I. Bytheway, W. R. (William R.) II. Johnson, Julia
    362.6

    ISBN 1-85628-102-7

Printed and Bound in Great Britain by
Athenaeum Press Ltd., Newcastle upon Tyne.

1992

WELFARE AND THE AGEING EXPERIENCE

This book is for John Evans of Llewitha, Swansea,
who was born in 1877, and who was the patron of the 1988 conference of
the British Society of Gerontology.

Contents

Acknowledgements

We are grateful to all the contributors for their patience and co-operation in the production of this book, to all those who contributed papers to the conference and who made it the success it was, to Carol Green, our conference co-organiser, to Anthea Tinker and more widely the BSG Publications Committee for their help in securing publication, to Kath Rees who has helped with much of the secretarial work, to Andrew and Richard Bytheway who prepared the camera-ready copy, and to Jo Gooderham and others at Avebury Press for their help and encouragement.

Editors
March, 1990

Preface

In a recent book review, Eric Midwinter (1990) commented 'we learn, with sinking heart, that the book is based on conference papers, than which no more effective means for producing shapeless and spatchcock publications has been discovered'.

The contributions to this volume are all based upon papers presented at the 1988 conference of the British Society of Gerontology (of which Eric is an active and valued member). In the light of his comments, we feel obliged to challenge his view and to proclaim the positive aspects of conference volumes. The problem is that readers typically, we suspect, go straight for those papers in which they know they have an interest, find that these leave them dissatisfied (because they already 'know' the answers), dismiss the rest as 'rubbish' and conclude that it is indeed one more shapeless and spatchcock publication.

Despite obvious limitations, conference volumes do have a number of distinctive and positive characteristics. First, for better or for worse, they exhibit the activities and concerns of a discipline at a point in time. The series of conference volumes that the British Society of Gerontology has published over the years, illustrates the changing character of gerontology in Britain.

Second, unlike the various journals of a discipline, the priority of the conference volume is, or perhaps should be, to represent the breadth of activities that are undertaken in the name of the discipline, rather than to maintain a certain standard or style. As a result, their variety - shapelessness, if you like - is one of their attractions. Collectively the contributors to this volume represent well the multi-disciplinary nature of British gerontology covering, as they do, nursing, psychology, social work, sociology, social anthropology, town planning and social policy. In editing this volume we have noticed all sorts of links that can be drawn between what initially appear to be unconnected contributions - there is shape if you look for it. We would urge the reader to follow suit and consider how one chapter might relate to another and, in the context of the changes proposed in the White Papers *Working with Patients* and *Caring for People* (DoH, 1989a and b), the possible future relationship between, for example, Mrs. Broadhouse, whose letter to the Guardian we quote in the first chapter, and the doctor, whose comment to Nolan was that 'the health services deny their responsibility for the disabled elderly and hide behind the medical model'.

Third, we see the publication of this kind of book to be the final act of a conference. Perhaps there is a certain mystery for readers who did not participate, but for those who did, or would have liked to have, the volume provides a tangible record of some of the efforts of, and exchanges between, those who contributed to the conference. Certainly we, as organisers and now editors, have learnt a great deal that is of direct benefit to our work as gerontologists.

Editors
March, 1990

1 A mixed economy of welfare and the ageing experience

Julia Johnson and Bill Bytheway

As we enter the 1990s, people born in the early part of this century are facing not only some of the expected personal changes of later life, but also changes brought about by government policy. The contributions to this book are based upon empirical research and, overall, concern the changing relationship between older people and the welfare state. The fact that the book, as a whole, does not prominently feature a critical examination either of aspects of this relationship such as poverty, ethnicity and ageism, or of the ageing experience itself, is perhaps an indication of current priorities in gerontological research. Much of the research here is driven by local policy and practice, and is funded under various government initiatives, local, national and European. Nevertheless, what does emerge from a close reading of the book is vivid evidence of how the nature of changes in the welfare state can directly affect the lives of older people and the relationships they have with welfare workers.

As we were preparing the final manuscript of the book, two items appeared in *The Guardian* which seemed particularly apposite. On 22 February 1990, there was a news item headlined ELDERLY GET WARD 'FIT FOR DEMOLITION'. A health authority, facing budget problems,

1

had decided to move twenty four elderly mentally ill patients into hospital buildings that three years previously had been categorised as fit only for demolition. The site of its present hospital had been sold to a supermarket chain for £29 million. A spokesperson for the health authority said that 'fit for demolition' had not referred to its suitability for 'use in the short run'.

The previous day, the newspaper had published a letter from Mrs. Broadhouse from Dorset which read:

> I am over 75. Apparently a doctor must visit my home once a year and ask impertinent questions as to my way of life so that he may assess continually my mental and physical condition and decide when the time has come to coerce me into selling everything I possess to pay for my incarceration in a private nursing home. ... For 70 years I lived through governments - Liberal, Labour and Conservative - and it never made much difference. They were all comfortably pragmatic, conservative (small 'c') democracies. Now I'm over 75 and that's all changed. I'm governed by a gang of fanatical dogmatists, all determined that everyone shall be continually assessed from the moment of his or her first day at school until the inevitable oblivion of a private nursing home. I don't like it.

(*The Guardian*, 21 February 1990).

We could not have hoped to find better examples of the connection between state policies and the well-being and ageing experience of older people (see also: Bytheway and Johnson, 1990). In 1989, two White Papers, *Working for Patients*, and *Caring for People*, have been published (DoH, 1989a and b). Both represent the promotion of a mixed economy of welfare that is favoured by the present government. They emerge from an ideological view which advocates 'rolling back the frontiers of the welfare state' and the development of internal markets within the statutory services. These broader political changes lead directly to the sale of hospitals and to letters such as that of Mrs. Broadhouse.

The first chapter, by **Davies**, places much of what follows in subsequent chapters in its organisational and ideological context. He uses the very powerful metaphor of 'trade and industry policies' which, he argues, underlies the Griffiths approach to community care (Griffiths, 1988). He suggests that the new frameworks and skills which will have to be developed as a result of the increasing commodification of services, have been largely overlooked in recent documents on community care. He points to the lessons to be learned from American experience and research.

Following a discussion of regulation and sponsorship, he argues that some older people face the risk of pauperisation if financing mechanisms are supply led rather than needs led. The majority would not be able to afford the more expensive forms of long-term care without eroding their assets and thereby risking pauperisation. He suggests that, following changes in the housing field where subsidies to council housing tenants are being phased out, the automatic subsidisation of other services may be questioned. He surmises that, in the absence of state subsidisation, insurance related devices will increase the ratio of income from charges to costs, and so reduce pressure on the social care budget, only if the income and assets of many elderly people grow substantially in real terms. This is crucial to the current debate regarding the competing interests of workers and pensioners (Johnson, Conrad and Thomson, 1989).

He recommends that financial brokerage should rest with care management at arm's length from the lead agency, and suggests that the value of influential and good brokerage, operating within a framework of policy that is established by a politically accountable agency, is one of the most important lessons to be learned from the United States mixed economy of welfare.

Davies points out that the long-term consequences, for publicly financed care, of the undocumented and unregulated growth in privately provided housing for older people, may turn out to be the problem of the 1990s, just as the publicly financed growth of 'for profit' residential care has been the problem of the 1980s. The typical public response of twenty years ago to the housing needs of older people was the provision of sheltered housing by local authorities and housing associations: a third of a million units have been completed over the last thirty years. Recently, however, there has been a dramatic growth of sheltered housing for sale, provided both by private housebuilders and by housing associations.

Its growth has been so rapid that little is understood about the local policy ramifications of such developments. The overall aim of the research reported by **Williams** is to document the expansion of private sheltered housing; to assess its contribution to meeting the requirements and preferences of elderly owner occupiers; and to evaluate the consequences of this growing sector, both for the development industry and for local authorities and housing associations. He, like Davies, points to the dangers to older people of developing services through market led structures rather than on the basis of need, and regrets the lack of attention given to these developments by health and social services departments. He too points to the threat of long-term pauperisation with increasing service charges and possible financial losses on the sale and purchase of properties (inevitable for some in a cycle of slump and boom). He also recognises the need for regulation to prevent abuse and malpractice. The new White Paper (DoH, 1989b) fails to acknowledge the significance of these developments for the future of community care.

Another aspect of the mixed economy of welfare is the provision of residential and nursing home care in the private sector and the increasing involvement of public sector workers in this area. **Phillips** presents an analysis of the part social workers currently play in the process of admitting older people into private residential care. The traditional role of the social worker, in regard to residential provision, has been in the assessment of a person's suitability and need for a place in a local authority home. Given the expansion of publicly funded places in private homes and the concomitant depletion of public sector resources, social workers have been forced to look for alternative provision and, as a result, to extend their role into the private sector.

Two hundred residents of private homes in Suffolk were interviewed, along with their relatives and significant professionals. Phillips looks at those people who received social work assistance and why they engaged their help. Only half of those on Department of Social Security funding received help from a social worker, and in many cases this help was minimal. She discusses the various roles of different participants in the process and, finally, the power they have, relative to others, to control and direct older people in their use of residential resources.

Davies found 'authorities whose headquarters have not developed clear strategies but whose middle managers clearly articulate what they see as the authority's decision not to co-operate with independent providers'. In keeping with this, Phillips found a lack of guidelines from headquarters on strategies to be adopted towards the private sector. She demonstrates that social workers, given a degree of professional autonomy in the context of unclear departmental policy, recognise when it is that they are making political decisions in regard to the care of their clients. Not surprisingly,

4

perhaps, it was hospital social workers who frequently engaged with the private sector. One may surmise that these social workers were less able to exercise their autonomy than their counterparts in area teams. If the White Paper proposals (DoH, 1989b) are implemented, social workers will be obliged to assume the kind of brokerage role anticipated by Davies.

Coles focuses on the problems currently facing the managers of local authority residential homes. It is frequently argued that, over the past decade, local authority homes for old people have had to adjust to an increase in the proportion of residents who are mentally infirm. Coles reports a study of practice in a social services department that has little formal segregation of such residents. He presents the all too familiar accounts given by staff of what looking after mentally frail residents means for them. His chapter amply illustrates Davies' point that many service providing authorities have become 'caught in the web woven by their past .... Some of the new ideas about care are incompatible with cultures and practices which are firmly established within departments'.

Coles suggests that successful local adjustment to the effects of the trend is both highly constrained, and conditional upon factors outside the immediate control of those in charge of individual homes. Mental infirmity is widely seen as a factor aggravating other threats to the quality of life in homes, notably inadequate staffing levels, architectural constraints on residents' privacy and the potential of social conflict in communal living. He discusses whether segregation of residents, assessed as being severely mentally infirm, would bring marked improvements for them and the remaining residents.

The research described by Coles in this chapter represents well the orientation of research driven by local policy. It is geared towards resolving particular management problems. Coles finds that the extensive research literature on residential care and mental infirmity has little to offer local policy makers. He is faced with the existing, limited resources of his Authority and sees their continuity as being outstripped by changes in circumstances and fashion. His predicament is perhaps that of many in-house researchers who are in the uneasy position of working in essentially ageist organisations. The difficulties facing older people regarding their mental health become 'problems' to be managed by professionals. As Kitwood (1988) puts it, this is all part of the 'technical

5

framing' which allows us to objectify the sufferers and thereby distance ourselves from engaging with them in a personal way. Mental infirmity then becomes a problem 'to be investigated and managed through technical skill'. The important lessons for the management of residential homes to be learned from research such as that of Lipman and Slater (1975, 1977), seem no longer to figure on the residential care agenda and this is a sad reflection of current policy and practice.

Coles mentions the importance that heads of local authority homes place upon opportunities to negotiate the admission to hospital of residents with whom they can no longer cope. Hospital managers recognise that people aged 65 years and over form their major client group and that, at any one time, this group occupies half of all hospital acute beds.

Victor's chapter focuses on the growing emphasis in the health service upon quick discharge rates from hospital. This has served to highlight the problem of 'bed blockers': patients who have been in hospital for more than four weeks and who, in the opinion of medical or nursing staff, no longer require the facilities provided in an acute setting. In one inner city health district, the delayed discharge of older people from medical and surgical wards was felt to be especially problematic. In large part, as Coles has demonstrated, the problem arises from the fear that afflicts many care agencies when faced with the challenge of meeting the needs of people with chronic and disorienting conditions. For the professionals responsible for providing services, the problem is transformed from one of delayed discharge to one of inappropriate placement.

To establish the scope and nature of the problem, Victor undertook a census of all older people on medical and surgical wards of two London hospitals. It was expected that the poor housing that is characteristic of inner city districts (not incidentally a concern of the housebuilding industry documented by Williams) would be a major cause of delayed discharge. Victor, however, found that there were far fewer delayed discharges than expected. This tends to confirm the view that the identification of problems such as 'bed blocking' and 'mental infirmity' are as much an indication of professional anxieties and inter-professional rivalries as they are of the behaviours of individual people. Using Lucas' terminology (Ch. 11), they are part of the idioms of the public accounts offered by service providers of the relationship that they have with their

6

clients (Hall and Bytheway, 1980). Davies' 'brokers' will have to be alert to the problems that this kind of professional behaviour presents.

Phillips' study indicates the important part that social workers might play in the alleviation of 'bed blocking', by moving those without alternative rehabilitation facilities into the private sector. Many doctors, however, would argue that one way to prevent this kind of problem ever arising is to develop day hospital provision for older patients. **Nolan** examines the current role of the day hospital and its relationship with other forms of day care. The relative failure of geriatric medicine to live up to its ideals of holistic and individually tailored care, is highlighted by his research on patterns of day hospital provision in North Wales. The study sought to elicit the perceptions of consumers (both patients and their informal carers) of the benefits of day hospital attendance and to explore the assumptive worlds of service providers. It demonstrates that existing definitions of legitimate day hospital function are dominated by the idioms of the medical model. This inhibits flexibility and creativity in responding to the demands of patients and their carers.

Nolan discusses the deleterious effects of the continued insistence of managers on discharge, and of the general failure by the gatekeepers of the day hospital service to fully recognise the importance of psycho-social influences on the well-being of users. He suggests that this, paradoxically, limits the usefulness of the day hospital in meeting its defined objectives. The White Paper on the health service (DoH, 1989a), echoed by that on community care (DoH, 1989b), promotes the power of market forces in determining provision. In that these forces, even more than in the case of community care, are to be articulated by brokers, and general practitioners in particular, then the 'proven effectiveness' of short term treatment in, and discharge from, the day hospital is likely to be strengthened yet further. In 1988/89, local authority residential provision decreased by 3.6 per cent and day care provision increased by 64 per cent (Age Concern, 1990), and so this chapter is highly relevant to current developments.

The chapters by Williams, Phillips, Coles, Victor and Nolan, all relate to the role of service providers in managing various kinds of possible change in the care system surrounding the older person in receipt of welfare services. Whether it is housing that can be bought to meet certain needs, residential or nursing home care, hospitalisation or day care, the

7

mixed economy of welfare analysed by Davies demands complex processes of negotiation regarding the needs of 'the consumer' and payment for the services provided. Coles, in particular, highlights the resistance to change that most people exhibit when wishing to remain as they are. By associating issues of finance with the complex set of relationships that characterise care systems, the mixed economy of welfare threatens to further confuse the already confused. If one could be confident that the market would be readily supplied with a range of commodities that would meet all needs, that the prices being asked were within the means of the consumer and that the agents (brokers) that the consumer might hire would provide an effective service in helping needs to be met, then choice could become a dominant force and older people might enjoy the satisfaction of controlling the ways in which their lives continue to develop (see Kautzer, 1988).

Moving on through this volume, the chapter by **Lansley, Pearson** and **Pick** takes us out of the welfare system and into that of retirement. They describe the findings of a research project which examines European policies and practice in preparing workers for retirement. There is still little provision in this field, and what there is can be related to structural factors: the existence of organisations specifically concerned with this work, the size of individual firms, and the location or responsibility for preparation for retirement courses within firms.

While it is possible to find examples of good practice in most countries, many courses provide little opportunity for participants to explore the issues which immediately concern them. Although the age of retirement is falling in many industries, and although de facto retirement following redundancy in later working life is increasing, courses still tend to cover issues associated with the health and social needs of old people. Few courses address the question of gender differences in retirement, and no one seems to be looking at the implications of retirement for migrant workers. They argue that community locations for courses for these groups are often more appropriate.

The authors are keen to have 'preparation for retirement' (PFR) move away from its 'traditional' role, which is focused narrowly upon the immediate needs of long-serving, full-time, male employees who are reaching statutory retirement age and facing a permanent cessation of full-time paid employment, and towards a more diffuse form of personal

8

development. However, this kind of move has to overcome the innate resistance of established practices. As Davies suggests, it may be more appropriate to begin with a new set of organisations. In regard to the needs that the Liverpool team have identified for a form of PFR for women, providers might consider the experiences of Bernard and Ivers and of Le Riche and Rowlings outlined in the following chapters.

A distinctive approach to helping older people adjust to the challenges of later life is described by **Bernard** and **Ivers**. The Self Health Care Project, based in Stoke-on-Trent, aims to encourage older people to take more responsibility for their own health care. It addresses the central issue of powerlessness which comes not only from a decline in income, but also from a poverty of access to the kinds of information and opportunities which might enhance health and well-being in later years.

They first describe the objectives of the project's Senior Health Shop and then detail the work of volunteer Peer Health Counsellors, of the project's outreach in residential homes and sheltered housing schemes, and of a telephone link scheme for frail housebound older people. A range of courses and self health care activities both for older people themselves and for professionals, make up a further component of the project.

They record the origins and development of the scheme, and provide pointers for others who might wish to set up similar projects. Their strategy would appear to be particularly appropriate to voluntary organisations, working in the community, that are keen to improve the access of particular groups of older people to effective health care. Their research found that contact with the project has proved effective in empowering individuals to take action to enhance their own health status.

Le Riche and **Rowlings** are concerned with the circumstances of women in later life. They describe an attempt to unite feminist and social work perspectives, in order to develop groupwork methods with older women. Two groups are described. The first, using an area office base, was aimed at women who live alone in the community; the second group was for women living in sheltered accommodation. In both groups the aims were to use the group to explore the experience of ageing, in relation to a range of broad themes such as redundancy, loss of family roles and women's experiences as consumers of welfare services.

The feminist literature emphasises the centrality of the concepts of empowerment and collaboration in women's groups, and both these issues had an impact on the groups' leadership styles. The chapter focuses on the importance of work which integrates macro and micro level experiences and thus creates links between the personal and the political. For example, the institutionalised ageism and sexism experienced by the women as part of their everyday lives was mirrored in the process of setting up and running the groups. Likewise, one can anticipate all sorts of matters that might be discussed in such groups arising directly from the implementation of the recommendations of the White Paper (DoH, 1989b). Such discussions, drawing upon shared personal experiences, might then lead particular individuals into taking specific actions regarding their care needs.

The chapter concludes with an analysis of the ways in which very different skills and perspectives from those of case management can be developed, in order that social workers become more effective. The challenge, which applies to all service providers, is to overcome the expectations that draw upon popular beliefs about what, for example, a social worker offers, what a social worker does, and most important of all what 'having' a social worker represents. They recommend the literature describing the use of an educational approach to issues of collaboration and empowerment. When linked to the findings of Phillips' research, the implications of their study for social work training, and in particular the forthcoming Diploma in Social Work, are immense (CCETSW, 1989).

Le Riche and Rowlings, and Bernard and Ivers, are concerned in different ways with the empowerment of older women. The particular circumstances of older women regarding employment, as Lansley, Pearson and Pick point out, have been sadly neglected in policies on pre-retirement and similar educational and preparatory courses. Dex and Phillipson (1986), following Szinovacz (1982), cite ample evidence to indicate that women are far from being a marginal or secondary workforce (see also Laczko, 1989). In addition, they demonstrate that the decision to retire is a serious one for both full- and part-time women workers. They discuss the neglect of older women that exists in employment research and policy development. Cooper and McGoldrick (1988), for example, in reporting on their research into early retirement in Britain point out that they were advised by the Economic and Social Research Council, the

10

funding agency, to focus on the retirement of men as the retirement of women was seen to be of a different character. Not disputing the explanation, one can still ask why they should first focus on men rather than on women.

Lucas examines the relationship between the family and older people by studying the character of intergenerational relations. Her research is set in Port Talbot where there was an in-migration in the 1950s and 1960s when the British Steel Corporation was expanding the steelworks. An out-migration followed from 1974, however, with the introduction of the first of a series of mass redundancies.

The data for the paper is drawn mainly from interviews with women, aged between 20 and 40 years, living on a large estate of council housing. She looks at aid, both financial and domestic, and how it flows not just from younger family members to the older generation but also from older members to the younger generation. She identifies conflicts in these relationships and discusses these in relation to the notions of responsibility, obligation and reciprocity. She concludes that the 'idiom' of reciprocity is used to minimise tension and conflict. An interesting aspect of her analysis is the way in which the concept of 'idiom' is used, and perceived of, as a regulatory mechanism. Her concern, therefore, is not so much with *why* people enter into certain sorts of dependency relationships (cf. Ungerson, 1987; Finch and Groves, 1983; Qureshi and Simons, 1987) but with *how* people explain what they do.

Given the importance of brokerage in the impending system of welfare, as indicated by Davies, given the experiences reported by Le Riche and Rowlings and by Bernard and Ivers, and given the evidence of the significance of professional attitudes provided by Phillips, Coles and Nolan, it is becoming increasingly important that attention is given to the ways in which ideas are expressed in care relationships and, in particular, how these are complicated and confused by dissonance between the generations.

Much of the received wisdom, both within the older generation and within the caring agencies, refers specifically to historical trends. Many views are legitimated on the basis of untested assertions about how things used to be. **Falkingham** and **Gordon**, like Lucas, are concerned with the relationship between class, the family and older people. With their invaluable data, they are able to examine the relative importance of family

11

and state over a fifty year period and, therefore, are in a unique position to comment upon historical changes during the course of this century.

They focus on two particular features of elderly people: the household composition and sources of income of working class older people. Data from the New Survey of London, conducted in 1928-30, is compared with pooled data from the General Household Surveys of 1979 to 1981. Their findings cast doubt on the importance of the family in providing financial support for older people in the past. The overwhelming and continuing importance of state income is clearly demonstrated. Insofar as it has grown, certain forms of state income, particularly occupational pensions and savings, have replaced income from employment and subletting. Furthermore, whilst changes in household composition over time have reduced co-residence, the authors also demonstrate that co-residence with the younger generation was not common in the 1930s. This brings into question the significance accorded to the co-resident extended family in times past, and thereby the capacity of the family to respond to calls for greater responsibility in the support of elderly people now.

A concept such as 'home' is central to popular images of the family, and to current health and welfare policies for elderly people, and yet its meaning remains vague. If we are to go beyond simple assertions that 'home' or a 'homely' environment is best for older people, then the concept must be examined in detail. **Sixsmith**, in the final chapter, presents the results of an in-depth comparative study of the meanings and experiences of home for three groups: elderly, employed and unemployed people. Through this, a number of key issues emerge regarding the significance of home in later life: the increasing importance of the home environment; the role of the home in affording instrumental and symbolic independence; and emotional attachment to home. These issues are discussed in relation to an experiential theory of ageing that suggests that the home becomes a prime focus of concern as people confront later life.

Here we are able to see connections to the points we made to open this chapter. Sixsmith shows how the idea that ageing is a problem leads to research on specialised accommodation rather than on 'home', and on functional support in residential care rather than upon the quality and character of life in such 'homes'. He has drawn upon the accounts that elderly people provide of their personal experiences, and the significance of this 'source' of insights into the care process cannot be

12

over-emphasised. He quotes Morgan (1983) to demonstrate how older people adopt a variety of strategies to avoid admission to an institution. This echoes the vivid sight of Thora Hird as Doris in Alan Bennett's play 'A Cream Cracker Under the Settee' (Bennett, 1988). Doris, having fallen, has the opportunity to engage the help of a passing policeman, but she chooses to keep quiet and remain on the floor of her own home.

We particularly value Sixsmith's discussion of the significance of 'coming into consciousness' in accounting for the attachment of older people to home. He argues that it is only when we know that we are approaching the end of our lives, that we become conscious of the immense significance of home. Echoing Lucas' line of argument, again, the way people talk about their homes is not just descriptive, it is constitutive. By talking about your home and what you do in your home, you actually constitute it as something more than, indeed something quite different from, just a 'dwelling' that was built to meet the demands of a market.

In conclusion, in reading this book, we might ask ourselves how it is that, at a time when a mixed economy of welfare is being energetically promoted, the experience of ageing and changes in later life is such that people like Mrs. Broadhouse should feel so threatened.

2 The 'Trade and Industry' metaphor and its relevance to the Griffiths Report

Bleddyn Davies

Reactions to the Griffiths Report (1988) have focused on the detail of the recommendations: how they affect various groups and occupations, and how they might be implemented. This is to examine the trees without seeing the wood.

The Griffiths Report proposes that the social service authorities should be the lead agencies in the delivery of community care. However, that it should be the social service authorities rather than some new community care authority (or indeed, the health authority in the case of the mentally ill) does not seem to be central to the Griffiths model for the improvement of efficiency. The separation of the responsibilities of the local lead agency into two sets, its 'trade and industry' policy functions and the performance of the 'core tasks of case management' is not explicitly made in the Griffiths Report. The latter have been discussed in detail in Davies and Challis (1986). This chapter focuses upon the former.

The case for using the metaphor

'Trade and industry policy' is in inverted commas because it is used as a metaphor. As such, it helps to suggest inconsistencies and gaps as we try to think through the implications of mixing the economy of the financing and production of community care. The case for applying it to long-term social care has yet to be fully made. It is a device for describing a class of activities which *are*, or *ought to be*, increasingly receiving the attention of social service authorities. 'Trade and industry policy' represents an important requirement to countervail the dangers of the continuing commodification of long-term care (Estes, 1979). The independent production and financing of the hard end of residential care, for example, is now well established. It would be astounding were it to be ended.

The metaphor differentiates between the traditional tasks of social service authorities (the financing, mass production and allocation of a narrow range of services consumed mainly by the poor) and the tasks increasingly stressed in a long series of government reports over the last thirty years (the development of local policies and frameworks for complex care systems). The latter have been seen as creating the conditions in which a mixed production and financing economy of welfare can work increasingly well, and is what I mean by 'trade and industry' policy functions. Its acceptance is part of a long slow cultural change in the organisations and cultures of local authorities.

The metaphor defines a proactive, not a reactive, role for the agency. This is important in a mixed economy which has many decision makers on whom sanctions are indirect and often weak. It works with, not against, constructive entrepreneurship whatever the source. Indeed, as long as it is monitored and there are effective policies to prevent distortions, it seeks to foster and even create entrepreneurship. Rather than rely on the command-control techniques of traditional public administration (Schultz, 1974), its orientation is to anticipate and correct potential failures in the market which might distort incentives to decision makers. It stresses incentives fitted to the values and motivations of decision makers in the way advocated in modern organisation analyses (Challis et al, 1988) and regulation theory (Majone, 1976). This encourages the agency to increase the variety of its means to influence behaviour and to develop new fiscal, regulatory and opinion forming devices. The history of American policy mechanisms for the payment and regulation of nursing homes provides some useful guidance to British policy makers, as well as illustrating again the inexorable growth in the repertoire of means.

The metaphor therefore encourages the lead agency to focus on where the market priorities presently are and where they will be: for instance, private sheltered housing schemes, continuing care retirement communities and adult fostering schemes. It is an antidote to the poison to which traditional local government cultures are particularly susceptible: the drift of the social service authorities into providing inadequately resourced standard services for the poor. It does not force alien policy formulae on local contexts and values: it reduces rather than increases the danger that services for a Sheffield or Coventry would be moulded upon those of a Berkshire or East Sussex and vice versa.

This chapter considers three examples which usefully illustrate the types of issue that require this 'trade and industry' approach. These are payment for service from public funds and regulation, sponsoring development in a mixed economy, and financial and brokerage mechanisms for user payment.

Payment for service from public funds and regulation

The theoretical analysis, empirical research, and programme experiments in the United States are impressive in quantity and quality (Davies, 1986). Although much of the work was published before the issues emerged most strongly in the United Kingdom, they are not well known here. The following are some of the conclusions that were drawn.

- Payment policies must provide simple and stable incentive structures focused on a small number of key goals. Stability is as important as simplicity. When payments were cut back and other features of the financial climate worsened, providers cut corners on quality.

- The key goals can, with benefit, differ between areas in response to contextual factors. However, the undesirable incentives of each set of payment policies must then be countervailed by other means such as regulatory devices. So, for example, financial support arrangements whose incentives are too complex to have beneficial effects must be simplified. Not only must the Gordian knot of social

16

security arrangements be cut, but arrangements for the regulation and payment for service must also be made within the framework of more general strategies which should vary between areas. Again they must be stable.

- Payment formulae should be based on expected costs that are fixed in advance for a class of institutions in an area rather than on retrospectively determined rates fixed by negotiation with individual institutions. These give more control over the rate of inflation of care costs, require smaller administrative outlays, and lower the probability of fraud and corruption. Generally, they provide better incentive structures. However, some of the differences in the consequences of payment systems depend on context; for instance, the degree of excess demand for services. In the long run, the fiscal system is a major influence on the cost structure of the industry, particularly if it is expanding quickly from a low base.

- Attention is increasingly being focused on payment systems that provide incentives to provide equitable access to persons who vary in the cost implications of equivalent care ('case-mix reimbursement'), to improve outcomes ('outcome reimbursement'), and to improve efficiency. Incentive reimbursement requires efficient and uniform auditing and monitoring. It is a complement of, not a substitute for, regulation.

- Non-fiscal policies can be more complex. Some US States have increasingly attempted to regulate processes and even outcomes, but have been hampered in doing so because they have inherited a framework with a focus on inputs. Again, the variety of devices to secure compliance with regulations, and the variety of inducements and sanctions were increased.

- A mixed economy of welfare requires more explicit contractual frameworks. Partly this arises because of the separation of the agencies that provide, finance and regulate care. Partly it reflects the increasing demands of those who consume the services and those who represent them. This accompanies their increased status as consumers and their expectations following a long period of greater power to make personal consumption decisions. The effect is to pay

17

greater attention to the law and to place more reliance on legal process. This in turn affects the choice of ends and means for a lead agency, the structures of regulatory organisations, and what can reasonably be demanded of agencies of different scale and geographical span. For instance, the State of New York came to separate the investigation and prosecution of offending suppliers from the provision of help for others to improve efficiency and standards. Regarding the former, attention had to be paid to collecting evidence in a form which would secure convictions in courts of law. Memories of Poulson should make United Kingdom authorities ever sensitive to the dangers of providing large profit opportunities without adequate monitoring and effective constraints.

There has been little British attention to this American theoretical argument and experience. Even the excellent analyses contained in the reports of Scott-Whyte (1985) and Firth (1987) do not draw upon it. Similarly Griffiths (1988), apparently not allowing the incentives generated by financing systems to distort local choices between residential and community based forms of care, ignores the consequences of the shift to the mixed financing and supply economy of welfare. In particular, the aspects of local 'trade and industry' policies that he ignores, include integrated local policies for payment for service, quality assurance, and the prevention of fraud, corruption and abuse.

Sponsoring development in a mixed economy

Many service providing authorities have become caught in the web woven by their past: their goals and achievements, their investment in human and physical capital and personnel policies. Meantime, ideas about the provision of services have moved on. For instance, writers now advocate forms of 'shelter with care' requiring expensive adaptations if not quite different formations of bricks and mortar (Willcocks et al, 1987). Some of the new ideas about care are incompatible with cultures and practices which are firmly established within departments. Some make the traditional turf boundaries between departments and authorities into real constraints on development. It may be easier to encourage the development of new organisations, rather than attempt to achieve change by managerial action within the existing structure.

Also local authorities have little financial slack. Many of their assets are poorly maintained and the costs of achieving the changes required are large new investments. In current circumstances, it can be advantageous to pay for the necessary investments indirectly, by having independent organisations actually create the capital and then offer the needed services under the provision of service contracts. In this way, high proportions of important social service authority budgets can be transferred to the income maintenance system.

In this context, changes in community care systems are being discussed in some of the same terms as in other areas of local government. Some authorities are thinking of creating organisations which would take over their entire stock of public housing. These would be legally at arm's length from the housing authority, but would be strongly influenced, if not effectively controlled, by it. No doubt those thinking thus are acutely aware of other policies which currently seem set to transform the relative power of central and local government: the halving of the proportion of local spending met from those taxes that are controlled by the authorities themselves with the introduction of the community charge, and the gradual extension of the principle of competitive tendering.

This creates opportunities for those who have in the past had little to do with social care. Consider one example. Maurice Phillips, until recently the Deputy Chief Social Service Inspector at the DHSS but now engaged by International City Holdings (Care Services), has argued that partnerships with the independent sector will be the only affordable way to achieve the required changes (Phillips, 1988). There are some authorities which are already considering the establishment of partnerships to create 'for profit' or 'not for profit' organisations which would take over services' capital stock, tap large sources of investment finance and property development expertise, and so change the nature of the services over a time period much shorter than authorities acting alone could do. International City Holdings is offering to 'manage the total development of schemes on behalf of statutory authorities with the help of other development companies' and to 'set up the financial structures in which this development will be possible', thereby saving authorities 'a lot of time' and 'a lot of complications', though not necessarily development costs. Phillips argues that compared with the existing servicing departments of local authorities (e.g. Treasurer's, Planning, Estates, and Architect's Departments), firms like International City Holdings bring a different perspective and wider skills in asset financing. They will gain the best tax and interest advantages, and will market sites across a wide range of organisations. The assets of individual facilities that are created within a single scheme might be owned by a variety of organisations; for instance, sheltered housing by commercial organisations, by specialist housing associations, or by companies in which the statutory agencies hold a share of the equity. There might be a division of function, with one organisation providing the property services and another the care services.

Care for those continuing to live at home is a natural target for those wishing to develop such arrangements, and the Griffiths Report (1988) is likely to stimulate this. The pressure to switch the balance from residential to community based care will give private providers of the former an incentive to diversify into the latter. Again with financial mechanisms to help, the managers of statutory home care services could in effect buy out the local authority provision, as has been done by some who run homes for the elderly. Not surprisingly, there have been few ambitious schemes. Judging from some interviews with directorates that we have been undertaking at the Personal Social Services Research Unit, many large authorities have not considered such matters at all. In others, the initiative is being taken by one or two people, often working without expert support within their departments. As might be expected, we have found authorities whose headquarters have not developed clear strategies, but in which middle managers clearly articulate what they see as the authority's decision not to cooperate with independent providers.

Financial and brokerage mechanisms for user payment

The Griffiths Report recommends the detailed examination of a range of options intended to encourage individuals to take responsibility for planning their future needs (para. 6.63). The case for improving financing and brokerage mechanisms for user payment is that:

- without better mechanisms for user financing, rising proportions of the population risk pauperisation;

20

- circumstances which should affect the selection and combination of financing mechanisms vary greatly, so that a disinterested brokerage service, based on an understanding of both financial mechanisms and long-term care, would improve the efficiency of the system;

- financing mechanisms now being developed are liable to cause long-term distortions, with the system being led by supply and financing structures, not by needs.

The threat of pauperisation

Increasing proportions of the elderly population are threatened with pauperisation because of long-term care costs. Higher proportions of elderly people will have income and assets substantially in excess of the levels at which they will be eligible for means-tested State services. However, a substantial proportion would neither be eligible for means-tested services, taking the supplementary pension level as the criterion, nor be able to pay for the more expensive packages of social care from their income alone. Walker and Hardman (1988, Table 9) calculated, from the Family Expenditure Survey for 1982, that 25 per cent of elderly households aged 75 or less, 14 per cent of those between 75 and 84, and perhaps 4 per cent of those aged 85 and more, had incomes of more than 140 per cent of the supplementary pension level. For most of these, prolonged utilisation of long-term care would eventually result in pauperisation.

Table 2-1 is based on a special analysis of the General Household Survey which permits analyses of households by type of area. It shows the proportions of persons living alone in 1980 and not receiving supplementary pension, for whom the payment for one of three care packages would consume the whole of their cash income, forcing them to spend down assets. It represents the proportion for whom the need for care might threaten eventual pauperisation. The three packages of care are assumed to be equivalent to the revenue costs of minimum, average and maximum local authority residential homes; namely £49, £77 and £120 per week respectively. The table also contrasts respondents according to whether they live in high or low status enumeration districts. As might be expected, the figures show that a majority of older people could not afford the more expensive forms of long-term social care without eroding their assets and risking pauperisation. It also shows that the proportions do not vary greatly between high and low status areas or between age groups, though the value of assets, and in particular houses, would probably be greater in the high status areas. Of course, the figures are for a general elderly population not for those at greatest risk of needing care. As the Family Expenditure Survey data quoted above and the other evidence used by Walker and Hardman (1988) illustrates, the proportion who are

Table 2-1 *The percentage of single person households in each age/sex/area group who are not in receipt of supplementary pension and who are unable to afford are at different cost levels*

Age	Sex	Area	Care cost level		
			Minimum	Average	Maximum
Under 75	Males	High status	63.1	65.3	67.4
		Low status	60.4	62.1	62.1
	Females	High status	67.0	71.2	71.9
		Low status	43.0	44.0	45.0
75 or over	Males	High status	54.8	54.8	54.8
		Low status	57.2	57.2	57.2
	Females	High status	67.4	70.4	71.2
		Low status	39.9	41.5	41.5

Source: 1980 General Household Survey

ineligible for supplementary pension and, therefore, not threatened by pauperisation is much lower among those with the greatest need for expensive forms of long-term care.

The threat of pauperisation is made greater (i) because the unit costs of care are likely to inflate faster than the general price level, and (ii) because the subsidies to social care services may be reduced. Care costs can be expected to rise, firstly because the numbers of persons entering the labour force will decline. A second reason is that long-term care is labour intensive, and increases in productivity may continue to be more difficult to achieve than in the economy as a whole. A third reason is that elasticity in the supply of women's labour may diminish as the proportion in employment increases. Although there are no econometric predictions

22

of the likely scale of these effects, a recent report assumes a rate of inflation of nursing home charges some 45 per cent greater than the general rate of inflation (Technical Working Group, 1987). The costs of care may increase further as pressure mounts to improve standards in existing facilities and to provide 'shelter with care' in ways more conducive to a better quality of life (Wagner, 1988).

Regarding subsidies, an increasing number of local authorities are recouping substantial proportions of their gross revenue out-turn from charges to consumers. For example, some services such as home helps now recoup as much as 25 per cent. There were some striking increases in the late 1970s and early 1980s, and we can expect them to have continued. Trafford increased its proportion from 5 to 13 per cent, Hereford and Worcester from 4 to 16 per cent, Norfolk from 5 to 19 per cent, Wiltshire from 8 to 20 per cent and Wakefield from less than 0.1 to 14 per cent. The pattern of variation between areas may reflect the propensities of authorities as much as the circumstances of home help recipients (Bebbington et al, 1989). These proportions look high in comparison with the home care services provided in some American states which have committed themselves to recouping costs through charges. According to the 1982 US Longterm Care Survey, only 12 per cent of disabled elderly people who were living in the community and receiving formal services paid for some of the cost directly from their own pockets. Among that 12 per cent, the median expense was $40 a month: less than £5 per week. However, some 10 per cent of those who paid made payments of over $400 per month (Technical Working Group, 1987).

Unit costs themselves will seem to be larger as local authority accounting systems are improved and fewer costs are hidden. Hidden costs are often much larger than (and not always highly correlated with) the revenue costs shown by local authority accounts. This is because of the omission of an allowance for the replacement cost of capital and the charging to overheads or other service heads, of resources used in the provision of care service. (See Davies and Challis, 1986, for services for the elderly; Davies and Knapp, 1988, for a general review; Knapp and Baines, 1987; Knapp, Bryson and Lewis, 1984, for children's services).

Griffiths proposes to restrict the financing role of the lead agency to 'meeting the costs of caring for people who cannot pay for themselves' and to covering the costs of case management. He argues that 'it seems right that those able to pay the full economic cost of community care services should be expected to do so' (para. 6.63). The subsidisation of the long-term care of all may not raise insuperable technical problems but, in a world in which local subsidies to tenants of council housing are being phased out, it would be surprising if the rationale of the automatic subsidisation of other services were not to be questioned. This is particularly so at a time when it is widely believed that resources should be concentrated more on the neediest.

It would be a mistake, however, to focus the discussion as if what matters is the present income and asset position of those at highest risk of need. As Griffiths (1988) makes plain, by locating his discussion of financial mechanisms in a section entitled 'long-term opportunities', the argument is about preparing for the quite distant future, not about the next few years. A failure to recognise this would prevent us from developing funded schemes such as (i) Individualised Medical Accounts (IMAs); (ii) tax favoured savings accounts that are tax free only if spent on medical or other long-term care; (iii) semi-funded types of long-term care insurance; (iv) continuing care retirement communities; (v) employee benefit options making it feasible to offer benefits at lower premiums because of the lower risk of adverse selection and the lower costs of marketing; and (vi) service credit systems (Sager and Sterling, 1982, and Cahn, 1986) whereby young elders might provide voluntary care and support in return for credits banked with the lead agency to be drawn on later as services are received. The arrangements have to be in place for some of these schemes thirty years or more before the funds will be called upon to make large benefit outlays. So we should be designing, assessing the feasibility, and demonstrating the practicability, of various financial mechanisms in a small set of experiments now.

It is not my intention to discuss these financing mechanisms here. Some analysis of American literatures and of the technical issues of using insurance related devices has already been undertaken (Davies and Goddard, 1987b). We are also working to estimate the affordability and other implications of various options. Based on the very preliminary work undertaken so far, it appears that, in the absence of state subsidisation, insurance related devices will *only* increase the ratio of income from charges to costs (and so reduce the pressure on the social care budget) *if*

24

the income and assets of many elderly people grow substantially in real terms.

The need for a disinterested brokerage service

The finances and ambitions of older people are as variable as their needs. They have, and increasingly will have, great variation in their combinations of incomes and assets. The appropriate combination of financing mechanisms for any one person should reflect this. It should also reflect how an individual would wish to use his or her income and assets, and this too will vary greatly. So the need is for a wide variety of mechanisms to help people to finance their own long-term social care, free from the threat of pauperisation (Davies, 1988). The financial mechanisms are not mutually exclusive. For instance, it might be sensible for a couple to agree (i) to pay an insurance premium of perhaps 5 per cent of their income and (ii) to buy an annuity with part or all of their housing equity. This will cover them for when the care bills come to exceed what their disposable income and insurance benefit would cover.

Thus one or a combination of mechanisms might be selected from the range to fit the needs of the consumer. Consumers might be provided with fiscal incentives to use them, the most obvious being some form of tax relief on premiums or contributions to a fund. Not all of such incentives would imply a current loss of tax revenue. For instance, the States of New York and Massachusetts are considering a plan to provide an incentive to persons to purchase long-term care insurance. The insurance would cover costs up to the average length of stay in a nursing home, and then, under the plan, their subsequent bills would be paid entirely by the publicly funded Medicaid. In this way long-term care would not force the older person to spend down his or her assets.

As this illustration suggests, from the perspective of the state, the best structure of incentives would be one that helps to target mechanisms in a way that concentrates public expenditure on raising the minimum standards of care. Estimates presented in Davies and Goddard (1987b) suggest that premiums might be affordable and worthwhile to substantial numbers, even without tax relief. However, the estimates possibly understate the premiums required and so overstate affordability, and the data suggests that the numbers of older people who are likely to see a policy to be good and affordable would be very sensitive to the level of the premium.

Because it is logical to develop a variety of mechanisms which can be arranged in combinations to suit the circumstances and wishes of individual consumers, selection will be difficult and the consequences of making a poor choice may be great. There is, therefore, a need to have expert brokers whose loyalty is to their clients. They also need to be accountable to an organisation that is responsible for ensuring the equity and efficiency of the community care system.

Brokerage advice should be given by those who have an imaginative understanding of the matching of resources to needs, and who have a thorough knowledge of the local system. Perhaps some aspects of their activities should be regulated by the local lead agency for community care. For these reasons, it has been proposed elsewhere (Davies and Challis, 1986; Davies and Goddard, 1987a) that financial brokerage should rest with care management (supply brokerage) in small specialised local organisations that are at arm's length from those allocating the large sums between broad budget heads within the lead agency itself. The greater the share of the market that is influenced by such brokers, the fewer the imperfections and the stronger the influence of the politically accountable lead agency on the overall pattern of supply and finance in its area. I believe that the value of influential and good brokerage operating within a framework of policy that is established by a politically accountable agency, is one of the most important lessons for the United Kingdom to be learnt from the US mixed economy of welfare.

Distortions due to supply led financing mechanisms

The amount of private purchasing power is already stimulating the development of mechanisms for financing long-term care, but these reflect the perceptions and interests of supply and financing structures rather than an understanding of long-term care needs. The long-term consequences for publicly financed care of the undocumented and unregulated growth in privately provided housing for the elderly may turn out to be the problem of the 1990s just as the publicly financed growth of 'for profit' residential care has been the problem of the 1980s. The private interests which are putting together and marketing current developments have little knowledge and experience of long-term care. It is vital that developments should be determined by policies aimed at meeting needs not by the sources of finance and supply. Without a form of brokerage, whose criteria are the best interests of the consumer mediated by the content of social policy, market failure already threatens.

Conclusions

Space prevents a systematic analysis of what would constitute the elements of the lead agency's 'trade and industry' policy. However, the examples included in this chapter demonstrate the need for the rapid development of new frameworks and skills.

It is a challenge which the scholarly skills of social administrators could help policy makers to meet.

3 Private sector provision of sheltered housing: meeting needs or reflecting demands?

Gwyn Williams

The post-war spread of home ownership, greater lifetime mobility, and a reduction in household size, has meant that the number of households headed by elderly people has increased substantially. Wholly pensioner households now account for a quarter of all households.

Considerable debate has been expended on the relative merits of age-segregated or age-integrated residential environments for older people. It has frequently been argued that the attraction of sheltered housing is that it provides good access to care, whilst at the same time fostering independence. Various public and private agencies provide accommodation either specifically designed, or of a size and price to appeal to older people (Table 3-1). This trend has been reinforced by the increased provision of newly built smaller units of accommodation in response to the increase in single person households in the population in general.

Specially designed housing, however, still accounts for only a small percentage of the stock of housing available for old people. The most

Table 3-1 *Specialised dwellings for the elderly, 1986*

Providers	Sheltered dwellings	Specially designed or adapted
Local authorities	281,000	297,000
Housing associations	92,000	21,000
Other public sector	3,000	6,000
Private sector	16,000	2,000
Total	392,000	326,000

Source: DoE estimates

marked change during the 1980s has been the shift from exclusive public provision, to a construction led private sector market of such housing. There has been pressure on new initiatives to provide sheltered housing at a reduced cost to the public purse, whilst guaranteeing greater choice. The growth of sheltered housing for sale, provided by both housing associations and private housebuilders has been the consequence, and this is the focus of the rest of this chapter (Williams, 1986).

Developments in housing policies for older people

Recently, many local authorities have sought to reduce sheltered housing costs by adapting the concept to 'sheltering at home', utilising dispersed alarm systems, peripatetic neighbourhood wardens, or funded 'good neighbour' schemes. An equally interesting development has been the growth of a variety of 'staying put' initiatives by housing associations and local authorities, which attempts to provide a house improvement agency service, and to give direct administrative and technical aid to older people (Wheeler, 1985; Tinker, 1984). Following early housing association experimental initiatives, this has now been taken up by the Department of the Environment. It has launched a national programme of fifty housing agency service schemes, a large proportion of which are focused on the needs of elderly households. Such approaches, based on the provision of an agency service, have generated considerable interest by focusing on the ability of elderly owner occupiers to pay for house improvements by borrowing on the security of their houses, and on helping them to gain their entitled statutory benefits. The 1989 Local Government and Housing Act proposes a further expansion of such services, and the introduction of means-tested home improvement grants is likely to be very beneficial to some elderly home owners.

Recently, substantial numbers of elderly owner occupiers have expressed a desire to live in specially designed sheltered housing, but have failed to meet the needs criteria defined by traditional public sector providers. Thus a buoyant housing market has begun to emerge in the last few years, which has resulted in the rapid growth of private sector construction of grouped dwellings designed specifically for older people. The sale of these dwellings has been promoted in terms of their advantages relating to security, freedom from external or ground maintenance, and the provision of emergency alarms and personal assistance. The demand is likely to increase steadily as younger age groups with higher levels of owner occupation reach retirement age (Table 3-2). One survey has estimated that if present policies continue, 80 per cent of elderly couples and 60 per cent of the elderly people living alone are likely to be owner occupiers within the next thirty years (Leather, 1990; Taylor, 1987; Hinton, 1987).

In mid 1982, the national estimate of the number of available sheltered units for sale was around 2,500. By 1989 this had expanded to around 60,000 units, a sixth of which were completed in 1988. Whilst over one hundred companies have become involved in building for sale to the elderly, the market leaders are undoubtedly McCarthy and Stone and

Table 3-2 *Percentage in owner occupation by age of household head*

Age of household head	1971	1986
Under 30	44	53
30-44	56	73
45-59	48	70
60-69	48	56
70 and over	45	49

Source: Social Trends, 1989

Anglia Secure Homes. Some of the major housebuilders have diversified their operations in recent years into extra care schemes on the one hand, and 'lifestyle' developments focused on the requirements of more active older people on the other. These schemes are largely found in the more affluent areas and suburbs, and attract elderly owner occupiers who possess higher incomes and more substantial assets. Thus the private sector's housing role is likely to focus on serving the needs of the relatively affluent, complementing the rapidly increasing private sector provision of residential and nursing homes (Housebuilder Supplement, 1988).

Under the 1980 Housing Act, registered housing associations may provide sheltered housing for sale at significantly less than market value. The aim is to help those unable to meet the full purchase price of privately developed schemes. A government Housing Association Grant subsidy, normally of the order of 30 per cent, enables owners of quite modest properties who have limited incomes, to purchase leasehold units. The objective is to enable an existing leaseholder to share in equity appreciation, and for the succeeding occupier to benefit from the reduction in price created by public subsidy. A survey by the National Federation of Housing Associations (1988) revealed that, nationally, there are 72 housing associations that are involved in managing these schemes. In total, around 4,000 units have been completed since 1980. As the pressures on housing associations to search for private finance has increased, a number have begun to promote privately financed full-equity sheltered schemes, and this trend is likely to increase.

Private sheltered housing for elderly home owners

Over the last decade, significant changes have taken place in Britain's housebuilding industry, and this has been reflected in the increasing importance of marketing within its operational structure and in the sophisticated targeting of developments upon specific client groups. The private sheltered housing market has taken over from the starter home market as the main growth sector within the industry. It is particularly attractive to developers, because elderly owner occupiers have ready access to equity, and are growing in number (Table 3-3).

However, although the retirement homes market was expected to be one of the few segments of the industry safe from the recession, it suffered

Table 3-3 *Performance of sheltered housing specialists*

		McCarthy and Stone	Anglia Secure Homes
Unit sales	1984	737	35
	1986	1769	107
	1988	2061	*600
Turnover (£m)	1984	22	1
	1986	67	5
	1988	150	37
Profit (£m) before tax	1988	34	8
	1989	7	-4

* Imprecise due to company takeovers.

Source: Company reports

a dramatic decline in 1989, selling a third less units than in the previous year. This was caused by broader housing market conditions spilling over: elderly people have been unable to sell their homes, and have been reluctant to reduce the prices being asked, since this is perceived to substantially affect the surplus capital intended to sustain future living standards. Thus, McCarthy and Stone, for example, were hit particularly hard. It experienced a drop of three quarters in its share value, with profit margins dropping sharply and the company selling only 1,571 units. In addition, it had 2,000 completed but unsold units, and a further 1,000 units under construction. Despite this setback, prospects for the industry in the medium term are sound, given the strong underlying demand.

The majority of elderly people are now entering retirement as owner occupiers. Their existing homes offer them the opportunity to realise capital and reduce living costs, by moving to smaller but specially designed units. High rates of owner occupation alone, however, provide an inadequate guide to market demand since the value of the property to be sold is crucial, and metropolitan fringe and coastal suburban areas provide the main market potential. The rapid expansion and the high profile promotion and marketing of sheltered developments, has led to advice about the development of good practice and possible pitfalls being given to elderly people (Age Concern, 1989), to developers and local authorities

(Housebuilders Federation, 1988; Hampshire CC, 1986; West Sussex CC, 1986), and to scheme managers (National Federation of Housing Associations, 1985; Housebuilders Federation, 1989). It has been realised that in addition to design features, the efficiency and integrity of property management is crucial to the success of such schemes: an area where housebuilders have had little previous experience. Additionally, both the development process and marketing have distinctive features, not found in mainstream housebuilding.

A number of specialist developers have concentrated on meeting the upper segments of the private sheltered market (from £100,000 to £200,000), either through new build or through the conversion of historic houses. The main focus, however, has been on the middle range of the housing market (from £50,000 to £80,000). Whilst McCarthy and Stone are a specialist builder within this field, volume housebuilders, regional companies and local builders have become involved. Originally, the market for retirement housing was perceived as being homogeneous, focusing predominantly on small apartments with on-site communal facilities and resident wardens. However, a recognition of the diversity of housing needs amongst older people has led to market segmentation, covering early and active retirement lifestyles, second retirement moves, and accommodation for those who are frail. Given the proliferation of such developments, it is particularly difficult to assess the exact size of the market in terms of completions or its eventual size (Williams, 1990a).

Marketing private sheltered housing is different from normal housing, in that prospective purchasers are usually trading down, and are more cautious and discriminating. Success is very dependent on the buoyancy of the local housing market. As local choice and price comparison has become available, a number of schemes that are deficient in terms of location, design or layout have proved particularly difficult to sell. Central to marketing has been a vision of carefree lifestyles based on financial and physical security and on independent living. Advertising slogans include 'Building for a Safe, Secure Retirement' and 'Security - Independence - Comfort'. McCarthy and Stone in particular, concerned with developing a national 'name awareness', advertises widely in specialist magazines and have their own 'house' magazine. Housing associations have had limited experience of marketing, being primarily committed to providing fair rent accommodation for family and special needs. However, their existing waiting lists offer a 'captive' market to whom approaches for lease sales can be made.

Local authority housing departments have generally adopted a positive attitude to the proliferation of sheltered housing schemes for sale, seeing them as a way of reducing the pressure on their own sheltered housing, and of improving the efficient use of the local housing stock. However, initial concern was expressed that schemes might encourage the in-migration of elderly people. The role of the local authority planning department has in the past been to consider the location, design and layout of proposed developments, and to consider the implications for local plans and for the local housing market. Some authorities, however, have been more positive, identifying suitable sites and encouraging appropriate development. In the case of South Ribble, Lancaster and Telford, for example, the district councils have been directly involved in building sheltered housing for sale on local authority owned land. Most local authorities sign Section 52 agreements with developers which places an age restriction on purchasers (usually 55 or 60 years of age). There is considerable evidence that local social services departments and health authorities possess a limited knowledge of the growth of private sheltered housing. Whilst this may not be a problem in the short term, in that new residents will initially make limited use of their services, it is clear that as the schemes mature and the residents age, increased demands may emerge.

Increasing co-operation between private housebuilders and housing associations in the provision and management of sheltered housing schemes has encouraged the production of a practice guide for housing association management committees (Housebuilders Federation, 1989). This argues that cooperation may be helpful, given cuts in mainstream rental programmes, as long as this did not conflict with overall housing association objectives. At least twenty-five associations currently manage private developer schemes. Such links, however, may create tensions in that the developer is primarily concerned with profitability, whilst the housing association's management role is with the needs of the elderly occupiers. The alternative management arrangement, adopted by many of the major private developers, is to set up their own management companies to administer such schemes.

Research into the local impact of sheltered housing for sale

Over the last two years I have been evaluating the impact of sheltered housing for sale (provided by private housebuilders and housing associations) on meeting the requirements of elderly owner occupiers; on local housing markets; and on policy within the development industry and within local authorities. While the study is relevant to the national context, the empirical research has been undertaken in four areas in the north west of England (Williams, 1990b, 1990c).

Through an analysis of local authority and housing association documentation, evidence has been collected on the extent to which sheltered units for sale complement or extend the existing provision of specialised housing for elderly people. It also examines links between such developments and the recent expansion of private residential and nursing homes. Particular interest has focused on the extent to which such developments have influenced local housing opportunities, and the strategies of the various organisations involved. Local impact has been studied through a survey of the characteristics of sheltered owners, their migration behaviour, aspects of consumer preferences and satisfaction and the recent housing history in relation to the nature of their previous dwelling.

The survey of sheltered occupiers

A central feature of the research has been a survey of sheltered owners in the four areas, undertaken during autumn 1987. Fifty-one completed and occupied sheltered housing schemes within the four areas were chosen as the sampling frame for our study. It was then decided to focus on four local housing markets, within which there were 21 schemes, providing 730 completed units. Having arrived at this sample, discussions were held with developers, housing associations and residential wardens, about the form and function of our approach to residents. Care was taken to ensure that the sensibilities of all concerned were properly protected. An overview of the results are discussed in this chapter. A fuller discussion of the results are discussed in the main publication arising from the work (Williams, 1990b).

Table 3-4 *Sample of sheltered housing schemes*

Type	Number of schemes	Number of interviews
Built for sale by private developer and managed:		
privately	6	185
by housing association	3	66
by local authority	2	44
Built for sale (privately financed) and managed by housing association	3*	61
Housing association leased	6	150
Local authority leased	1	9
Total	21	515

* Including one housing association loan stock development

Of the 730 sampled units, 67 were empty and, of the remaining 663, there were only 58 outright refusals of co-operation. The 90 other non-respondents related to bereavement, ill-health, being away on holiday, in addition to a number who appeared to be in, but were unwilling to come to the door. Of the 515 elderly households, 295 were in private developer schemes, 211 in housing association schemes, and nine respondents in a local authority leasehold scheme (Table 3-4).

Socio-demographic structure

Three quarters of all respondents were living alone, and three quarters of all interviews were with women who were heads of households. In addition, nearly two thirds of all respondents were widows or widowers, with only one quarter of all households being married couples. The median age of respondents was 76 years. The younger average age of those occupying housing association schemes (74 years) reflects the often minimally sheltered nature of many these schemes: no resident warden or communal facilities. Twelve respondents were under 60 years (the youngest being 57) and there were 22 over 85 years (the eldest, 93 years). Indeed, 44.5 per cent of all respondents were over 75 years of age.

Whilst self assessment of health is clearly of limited clinical value, it does give some insight into personal perceptions relating to both welfare and independence. Only 12 per cent of respondents considered themselves 'not well', but respondents living as part of a couple tended to see their partner's health to be poorer. There are important issues for the future concerning the management of such schemes as respondents age 'in situ', and as the schemes themselves mature: only a tenth of all respondents had considered a further accommodation move.

Housing history

Almost all respondents had lived in their present accommodation for under three years. Only now are there sufficient schemes within specific local housing market areas, for intending occupants to have some choice in relation to location, price and range of facilities. Consequently, whilst 61 per cent of all respondents had moved under ten miles, as many as one fifth had moved over fifty miles. Those who had moved furthest tended to be in schemes provided by private housebuilders. This may be due partly to the type of market niche being targeted by the private sector, and partly to the more localised nature of housing association marketing and advice.

As would be expected from a group of fairly affluent elderly owner occupiers, the overwhelming majority of occupants (78%) previously occupied detached or semi-detached housing, the majority of which (63%) had at least three bedrooms. Thus the move into sheltered accommodation also represented a change in lifestyle, and this has major implications for the use of private sector housing stock. However, it is interesting to note that three tenths previously occupied bungalows, and a further tenth lived in flats, suggesting that for many this was their second move in retirement. Whilst the median length of previous residence was nineteen years, nearly a third of all respondents had lived in their previous home for under ten years. One fifth had occupied their housing for over thirty years and they tended to be in housing association schemes.

In terms of the financial issues raised by the development of sheltered housing for sale, it is instructive that nearly half of all previous homes were sold for under £30,000, and only 14 per cent for over £45,000. Further work is currently being undertaken on the use of home equity in such moves, and the existence of financial surpluses that become available to the individual as the result of a move. Overall, one seventh of all households appear to have generated asset losses as a result of such transactions, and this is particularly the case with respondents who had bought into full equity schemes. One fifth of all such respondents had to use assets in addition to their previous home to pay for their new accommodation. This raises issues relating to the future financial wellbeing of these residents. Such asset losses will increase their anxiety about their ability to cope with escalating management and services charges, and possible health care requirements in the future.

The decision to move

The major reasons for moving into sheltered accommodation related to problems concerning the use and maintenance of their previous homes (36% overall), the wish to live nearer to established family connections (22%), and concerns relating to frailty and health (18%). Having decided to move, it is clear that, whilst bungalows and flats were important considerations as housing options, one fifth had considered renting sheltered accommodation. This is some measure of the reduction of pressure on such stock resulting from the growth in the market of sheltered housing for sale. However, over two thirds of those who had actively considered renting accommodation, had perceived housing association rather than local authority accommodation as satisfying their requirements.

In considering the merits of sheltered schemes for sale, three fifths of all respondents had only considered the scheme that they had moved to, with the main source of information coming from the family (35%), site notices (24%), newspaper advertisements (16%) and friends (12%). Thus it is not surprising that much of the marketing of schemes is targeted not on older people themselves, but on their families. It is, however, highly significant that over half of all respondents had received no advice from anyone prior to purchasing their sheltered dwelling, and this is of considerable importance in terms of the legal and financial issues associated with the further development of this segment of the housing market.

Resident satisfaction with sheltered housing

Given the relative infancy of such developments, with resales only beginning to test the buoyancy of this segment of the housing market, it is premature to come to firm conclusions on overall resident satisfaction and the sustainability of the market. Indeed, elderly households generally tend to be more satisfied with their accommodation than other age groups, so it is not surprising that the vast majority of sheltered owners were satisfied with their apartments, stressing accessibility, security, lack of maintenance responsibilities and the quality of social interaction.

In regard to design features, the main criticisms related to car parking arrangements and the lack of suitable internal storage space. In terms of management services, the quality of gardening maintenance appeared to be a major area of dissatisfaction. In contrast, residents were generally satisfied with wardening and communal cleaning arrangements. Over three quarters of all respondents had never had to use the emergency alarm system. However, in terms of overall service charges, over a quarter of all respondents felt that they received poor value for money.

One third of all respondents owned a car, with nearly half of car owners using their cars daily. Overall, 55 per cent of respondents used public transport on a weekly basis, and this is further evidence of the general level of mobility amongst these households. In addition, over three quarters of all respondents used local shops several times weekly, and only 8 per cent of respondents used local shops less than once a month.

Social interaction and elderly lifestyles

In regard to the family, one quarter of all those surveyed had no children, whilst a further quarter had only one child. However, of the three quarters of responding households with an immediate family, 72 per cent had children living within a ten mile radius. Even so, in a fifth of cases where households had immediate family, the nearest child lived at least fifty miles away. The move into sheltered accommodation has generally been perceived positively in terms of family links, with nearly two thirds of those with children receiving visits at least weekly. However, a quarter had visits less often than monthly. Contacts with both family and old friends were aided however by the telephone, with only twelve respondents not possessing one.

There was a surprisingly low level of visits by both public and private services to the schemes, with the home help being the most frequent visitor. Indeed, only 9 per cent of households paid for any public services, and only 8 per cent paid for private services. However, issues concerning the delivery of welfare services will undoubtedly increase in importance as the schemes mature, and as owners progressively age. A sharp increase in demand for social care during the 1990s may mirror the explosive growth of these schemes in the 1980s.

Within individual schemes, social interaction appeared to be well developed, with the majority of respondents either visiting neighbours, or being visited by them, at least on a weekly basis. However, only one seventh of respondents had daily contact, and over one quarter claimed that they paid no visits and were not visited by neighbours. Thus many remain relatively socially isolated within this group living arrangement. Whilst a third of all respondents claimed that no social activities were organised within their schemes, the vast majority of residents participated where such activities were available. In regard to the extent to which the move into sheltered housing was perceived to have had an effect on feeling lonely and losing self-esteem, one quarter felt less lonely as a result of the move, but one eighth felt lonelier and more socially isolated. Thus it is clear that even within such potentially supportive living arrangements, many remain isolated.

Conclusions

This paper has traced the development of an important new sector within Britain's private housebuilding industry, and noted a new dimension in the work of housing associations in their relationship with private developers, both in the management and in the provision of sheltered units for sale. Lively market demand from older owner occupiers has provided an attractive new avenue for the efforts of the housebuilding industry. It has generally been welcomed by local authorities as a way of improving the utilisation of existing housing stock, while simultaneously reducing pressure on public sector provision.

Concern has, however, been expressed at the vulnerability of older people to the operation of market forces. There is, for example, some evidence that, as a result of the strong marketing efforts of some companies during the period of buoyant demand in the mid 1980s, many owners may have paid excessively for extremely small, if well appointed, apartments. Indeed, when service charges, ground rent and other costs are taken into account, financial outgoings are often not reduced by such a move, and some owners are anxious about their capacity to meet rising costs in the future. Welfare agencies are additionally concerned at the capability of the private sector to develop extra care support systems for the increasingly frail. Similarly, many housing association management committees have become concerned about maintaining a proper balance between meeting the social needs of special groups and responding to market demands.

Thus social welfare issues associated with these developments may become a major area of policy concern during the 1990s. They will raise fundamental questions for traditional care agencies, about the extent to which they should and can participate in the provision of welfare services for a client group with considerable potential needs, but whose accommodation requirements are being fuelled by market processes. So far, there is little evidence that the health and social services have given due consideration to the major challenges for their activities that these developments present, as both schemes and residents progressively age over the coming years.

Acknowledgement

This research has been undertaken as a result of the award of a research grant from the Economic and Social Research Council, complemented by a small award from the Joseph Rowntree Memorial Trust.

4 The reaction of social workers to the challenge of private sector growth in residential care for elderly people

Judith Phillips

The traditional role of the social worker in the admission of elderly people to residential care is the assessment of the person's suitability and need for a place in an old people's home, along with the practicalities of the admission such as finding a suitable home, managing the transition from home to residential care and helping the elderly person to settle in.

It was natural, then, when an increasing number of elderly people sought help to enter the vastly expanding private sector of homes, that social workers should extend their role and apply their skills to the process of admission into private residential care.

Little research has been carried out, however, on the reaction of social workers to private sector growth and the increasing responsibility placed on workers in the social and health services to help elderly people in their transfer into an alternative sector of care. In some respects, social workers have been forced to work within the private sector as a result of the increasing numbers of people seeking their help following the change of funding arrangements in November 1983, allowing an influx of state supported elderly people to enter the private market. The move into the market system was not encouraged in any planned, systematic way or governed by policy initiatives and as a result some social workers have acted autonomously.

In contrast, the social services departments have responded to their legislative function of registration by promoting an ethos of pluralism. What such 'partnership' of common interests means in practical terms of a working relationship between social workers, their clients, families and home owners is far from clear. This is demonstrated by the analysis of the social workers' role and their reactions to private sector growth presented here and apparent in the wider research literature. For example, Willcocks et al (1987) illustrated this in their study of the registration process and role of the registration officer.

This chapter attempts an analysis of the social worker's role in the process of admission into private residential care. The context in which the research took place is outlined. The part that social workers played in the process of admission in relation to relatives and others, and how they played that part, is described. Why elderly people received a variable level of service and why social workers withdrew or participated in the private sector is discussed. Finally, consideration is given to the consequences of social work activity in the private sector in the light of the extra skills and knowledge that are needed if they are to continue to be valuable resources to elderly people and their families.

The role of the social worker was found to be varied and complex and, in some instances, it varied according to the individual social worker's personal perspective of the private sector, and according to his or her interpretation of what agency policy means in practice.

The research context

A three year research study looking at the critical steps in the journey into care and the various processes operating in the admission was undertaken between 1985 and 1988.

Two hundred elderly people who entered thirty-nine private homes in Suffolk in one year, were interviewed in relation to their experience of the admission process. A series of interviews were also carried out with relatives and professionals identified by these elderly people as being significant in this process. Forty-two social workers who were involved in the admissions were contacted by telephone and asked to describe their role, extent of involvement and attitude towards the private sector. In addition, eighteen other social workers who were initially contacted by families or the elderly person and who had withdrawn without further involvement, were interviewed to find out why they had done so.

Although not considered in this chapter, a comparative study of 120 elderly people entering local authority homes also took place. The samples were selected in the same way for comparative purposes (Table 4-1).

Table 4-1 *Composition of sample interviewed*

	Private	Local authority	All
Resident	200	120	320
Relative	120	52	172
Professional	80	60	140
Home owner	39	19	58
	439	251	690

Significant people in the process of admission to private homes

The first question considered is the extent to which social workers were involved in the process. In contrast with an admission into local authority care, there is no requirement placed upon those seeking a place in a private home, to engage a social worker in the process of admission. However, although direct communication between elderly people and home owners is possible, only 11 per cent of the sample acted independently in that they bought directly into private residential care themselves. Table 4-2 shows that social workers were not the most significant source of help for those needing assistance in entering private care.

Table 4-2 *Significant people in the process of admission*

	Number	Percentage
Relative	120	60
(offspring		44)
Social worker	71	35
Nurse (DP/DN/HV/CPN)	31	15
Other	32	16
Client alone	21	11
Total (= 100%)	200	

Relatives

The majority of elderly people were helped by relatives, mainly sons or daughters who had generally played an important part in their lives prior to the process. A number of elderly people were dependent upon their relatives in terms of mental, practical and emotional support. They were also dependent on them in respect to their future care, as it was often the inability of relatives to continue in the caring role that had initiated the process.

Relatives were also influential in deciding which private home was best suited to the elderly person, and they frequently took the lead in negotiations with home owners. In some cases they built up a considerable body of knowledge about homes in their area.

Social workers

A total of seventy-one admissions to private homes (35%) involved the help of a social worker. The help provided, however, varied enormously. They fell into five broad groups (Table 4-3). In the first, in the case of eighteen admissions the social worker either provided basic information, generally financial, and gave the enquirer a list of private homes in the area, or participated further by considering with the elderly person the advantages and disadvantages of all the options - at this point there was no further contact. In the second group, fourteen elderly people were recommended a private home. In the third, eleven were assessed for a place in a local authority home but the lack of vacancies restricted a continuing role for the social worker. In the fourth group, four elderly people were also assessed for public sector care but were then recommended a private home.

At the other extreme in the fifth group, the social worker played a significant part throughout the admission process of twenty-four elderly people. This involved help with decision making, negotiation with the owners on the client's behalf, assisting the client through the transition period and the practicalities of the admission itself.

Table 4-3 *Level of social work contact in the private residential care admission process*

Contact	Number
No involvement	129
Marginal involvement (eg list given)	18
Recommendation of home (no follow-up)	14
Assessment for care (no follow-up)	11
Assessment, list given, home recommended	4
Full participation - assessment, placement, follow-up	24
Total	200

Overall, then, social workers played only a marginal role in the process of admission into private residential care. Of the 200 elderly people entering private homes, only 12 per cent received a significant level of assistance from a social worker throughout.

Non-involvement

Table 4-4 shows a breakdown of why social workers were not involved in admission. Some social workers held political values and attitudes opposing privatisation. Although small in number, they held strong views and demonstrated this by withdrawing their service irrespective of whether a person was in need or not. One social worker, for example, said:

I don't want to deal with the private sector. Personally I disapprove. It doesn't offer safeguards, consistency, protection or security, just profit.

Another social worker said:

I shy away from the private sector due to my personal politics. I don't favour privatisation and I've resisted all the policy moves.

In some instances social workers saw their role to be limited to the public sector alone, and withdrew their involvement when faced with a lack of public sector resources to offer. They did not see their role extending to the private sector.

Table 4-4 *Reasons why social workers were NOT involved in private sector admissions (number of admissions)*

```
Social worker withdrew after first contact because:
  (i) of their political values                      8
 (ii) they saw their role solely in the state system 8
(iii) elderly person's family were involved          2

Social work service was:
  (i) ignored by families                            6
 (ii) by-passed by other professionals               8
(iii) not requested by elderly person               97
```

Total	129

Two social workers felt that they should not be involved in the private sector if relatives were available to help the elderly person. Intruding into a private arrangement between families and home owners was not seen as a legitimate role for them. One said:

If the family are keen on private care after I've explained the options then they can go away and explore it themselves. We tell them about it but it's a private arrangement.

The above reasons for withdrawing from a relationship with the private sector illustrate that some social workers were *not* taking on what the British Association of Social Workers terms 'an independent voice on

47

behalf of the client'. Nor were they 'enabling the client as far as possible to make a personal decision which might be different from that made by relatives or friends' (BASW, 1984, p. 9). Arguably, this group of social workers, by withdrawing their involvement as a result of their personal opinions, were acting as barriers and were depriving elderly people of an informed choice.

A total of ninety-seven elderly people did not recognise the need for a social worker and, along with some families, chose to ignore the social worker in the process. They could not see the social worker as making any helpful contribution, particularly if there were no vacancies in local authority accommodation. One social worker said:

> I was involved in discussing future plans and I assessed her for different options, but they didn't look at any homes with me. As the daughter presented it to me - *fait accompli* - they had found a vacancy.

Other professionals, particularly in the medical field bypassed the social workers, again because they saw the role of the social worker to be confined to the public sector alone.

Active involvement

The discussion now turns to the forty-two social workers who took an active role in the private sector - whether by providing a list, recommending, assessing or by fully participating in admission (Table 4-5). The questions considered are first why social workers took on a role,

Table 4-5 *Reasons social workers gave for being involved in private sector admissions*

	Number
Preference for private sector	18
Pragmatic reasons	17
No family involved	2
In best interest of elderly person	16
Knowledge of particular home	10
Total	42

48

however marginal, in relation to the private sector and second how they interpreted agency policy in this area.

Reasons for involvement

Five groups of social workers were identified regarding the reasons they gave for being involved in the private sector. The first group who were actively participating in the private sector held views favourable to it. One, for example, said:

> I prefer to use the private sector, it suits my politics.

Others found it a much more flexible resource as they could admit elderly people without delay free of the hurdles of bureaucracy. Sixteen of the eighteen social workers in this group were based in hospitals.

Although adopting an active role within both sectors, the second group of seventeen social workers expressed mixed feelings about their role. They considered themselves to be forced into this position through the lack of resources within their own sector of operation. They viewed themselves first and foremost as gatekeepers to the local authority system but, faced with a lack of available beds and a long waiting list, they turned to the private sector for a quick solution. One said:

> We are forced to use the private sector a lot. In principle we don't like it, but when people can't go home from hospital and have to wait for Part III, then it's often the case of having to look to the private sector, particularly if they are married.

These social workers felt they were engaged of necessity in a relationship with home owners, one that was artificial but necessary through the lack of appropriate alternative resources.

Where no families were involved, the third group of two social workers acted as advocates on behalf of the elderly person. Of the sixteen social workers in the fourth group, about one in three of the sample, felt that they should be involved with elderly people simply in order to meet their needs in the best or most appropriate way. They held no preference for one sector or the other, and in the case of admissions to private care this was seen as the most appropriate.

Finally the fifth group of ten social workers used the private sector when they knew the elderly person could be channelled into a particular

49

home. The social worker had developed a good relationship with a number of private homes and had built up a network of contacts which could be tapped when needed. Some patronized what they saw as good homes and boycotted the bad. Many had a good rapport with some homes which worked to benefit their clients. They knew when a home could cope and, that if there were any difficulties, the home owner would contact the social worker.

Overall, then, most of these social workers were actively engaging their skills outside the realms of the public sector and taking on new roles as well as traditional ones. For example, the majority, whatever their views, when contacted in respect of a potential private home admission, created the possibility of choice for the elderly person by at the very least informing him or her of the existence of a private home. Only a small group of eighteen social workers were arguably depriving elderly people of this possibility.

The variability in role and level of involvement, however, meant that elderly people received an unequal service. Whether elderly people were given a choice or not depended on the allocated social worker's perception of their role in the private sector. Not only this, but also on what they thought their agency's policy was on working with the private sector.

Interpretation of agency policy

Private sector growth has also focused attention on the autonomy of social workers, and has challenged the relationship between this and agency objectives. At the time of the research, there was no translation of the agency policy of pluralism into practice guidelines for social workers. Few social workers knew of this policy and, where they did, there was a lack of consistency in their knowledge of what it was in regard to the private sector. Half believed there was an unspoken agreement that social workers should not place elderly people in private homes, and the other half believed that pluralism implied that they should actively promote it by participating in both sectors of care. As a result elderly people and their families could receive conflicting messages from the same agency.

Conclusions

It is clear from this research that overall social workers played only a marginal role in the process of admission to private care. Where they were involved, this varied according to individual perspectives of private homes and to individual interpretations of agency policy. Given that the Social Services Department had not translated its policy of pluralism into practice guidelines, social workers could exercise a considerable degree of autonomy in their dealings with the private sector.

The Government's commitment to privatisation has been reflected in the reports of Griffiths (1988) and Wagner (1988). The Firth Report (1987) looked specifically at the issue of public sector involvement in the private market. The screening of applications for admission into private residential and nursing home care, particularly for people seeking public funding, has been welcomed by those who feel that there should be tighter regulation of the process of admission. They would argue that the present 'open ended' system of funding provides 'perverse incentives' for residential care as opposed to care in people's own homes (Audit Commission, 1986). The Firth Report presumes that it will be social workers who would assess the need for admission to residential care where state funding is sought.

If there is an intention to provide a fair and objective system of assessment which offers genuine choices and if social workers are to play a key role in this, then the autonomy that they currently have would have to be restricted. Whatever their political views, they would have to become more knowledgeable about the whole spectrum of different resources that the private sector has to offer and, by necessity, extend their involvement with private homes. In addition, they would be required to fully engage in the admission process and to monitor changes after admission - offering appropriate alternatives where necessary.

Clearly the increased involvement of social workers in this field of activity would have considerable financial implications. In the Suffolk study, 34 per cent of those entering private residential care were state funded, but only half (48%) of these engaged the help of a social worker. The possible savings accruing from tighter control of publicly funded admissions may easily be outweighed by the additional costs of assessment for the other half. Add to this, the findings of Bradshaw and Gibbs (1988) who showed that, when account was taken of existing services, only 6.6 per cent of elderly people were found to be inappropriately placed in private homes and did not 'need' to be there.

In order to provide a fair service for all, the objectives of assessment would need to be clarified. Without this, the possibility of a fair system which offers all elderly people the same prospect of appropriate care would not be possible. Rather, there would be a two tier system of well-resourced care for those with the personal means to pay for it and an under-resourced system for those who cannot. The latter would be based upon multiple assessment, and bureaucratic hurdles dictated by both market forces and professional judgements.

5 Continuity and innovation in residential care: adjusting to mental infirmity in local authority homes for the elderly

Oliver Coles

Providing for mentally infirm elderly people and planning improvements in residential care are two activities that are particularly taxing and controversial in the field of local authority social services planning in the United Kingdom. When the two are linked the issues become yet more intractable. Essentially this is because mentally infirm people are particularly reliant upon the continuous supervision which residential care offers. Yet traditional patterns of life in local authority homes are threatened by a substantial presence of residents with this condition. At the same time these patterns are themselves under attack as being incompatible with contemporary norms relating to the life styles of elderly people. The Wagner Report (1988), for example, summarised research that has demonstrated the undesirable outcomes for residents of traditional practices.

The research discussed in this paper examined how the homes of the

Social Services Department in County Durham have adapted to the growing presence of residents with substantial degrees of mental infirmity. The policy context of the research was a need to decide whether some or possibly all mentally infirm residents should be formally segregated from other residents in the interests of both groups. It became apparent from reviewing the literature that this is not a self contained technical question. Instead, prescriptions are highly context specific, a fact underlined by the radical implications of the recent White Paper on community care (DoH, 1989b). Although there have been many studies of the segregation or integration issue, it was found that these did not offer the kinds of guidance that was needed to develop services appropriately in County Durham.

Research design

The literature review yielded two distinct messages. One, based almost exclusively on North American literature, is that it is possible to identify optimal conditions, in terms of resident mix and service inputs, for both therapeutic segregation and therapeutic integration. The other, arising from an influential set of British studies beginning with Townsend (1962), is that segregation is undesirable. British service managers have been placed under considerable pressure to make full integration work, in the belief that it must be more humane than the segregation graphically described by Townsend and by Meacher (1972).

For example, Evans et al (1981, pp. 9-11) concluded that 'under present conditions ... a proportion of around 30 per cent confused ... can be tolerated'. This was not particularly helpful in developing policy in Durham, partly because the heads of homes surveyed in the present study did not agree with it, many seeing it as unduly mechanistic, and also because it did not provide guidance in the situation where the proportion exceeded this figure.

In the absence of sufficient examples in Durham of segregated settings, it was decided that the research should focus upon inter-home variations in the degree of success in formal integration. Clearly if success was eluding homes or was being bought at an unacceptable price, such as very extensive informal segregation or the use of unacceptable means of restraining residents who are perceived to be disruptive, then a general case for segregation could be made.

It was also felt that the dynamics of individual homes were important, and consequently that what was needed was a study undertaken at more than one point in time, one which allowed the study of the adjustment of homes to changes in resident mix. Prominence, it was felt, should be given to a model which treats the home as a social system. It was hypothesised that where adjustments to changes in resident mix are insufficient, whether due to organisational or other factors, then stress is produced in the system. For example, although designed for an approach to home regime and life style which is quite alien to current thinking, the buildings of most of the local authority homes in Durham are sufficiently new to be sound and would be inordinately costly to replace.

The results presented here therefore relate to interaction at the local level between the continuity of service provision and changes in resident mix. Although intended solely to assist in the development of services in County Durham, the results will be of interest to providers of residential care elsewhere.

Data sources

Data were obtained from three main sources. Firstly, in December 1986, a questionnaire survey was sent to the heads of all the forty-four homes run by the Authority. Secondly, observations were made on personal visits to a sample of these homes in order to explore layout and amenities and to talk to staff. Finally, a biennial day census of all the permanent residents of the homes was undertaken. This was first conducted in 1977 (Coles, 1985) and thus provides a time series that is unusually long for data of this kind.

Change: the growing presence of mental infirmity in homes

The emergence over the decade 1977 to 1987 of growing numbers of residents with a substantial degree of mental infirmity is traced in Table 5-1. There has been an increase from well under 10 per cent to nearly 17 per cent in the proportion of residents judged by the heads of the homes to have a 'severe' mental state. At the beginning of the decade, just over half of residents were classed as not being of a 'normal' mental state. By 1987 over two thirds of residents suffered from some degree of mental infirmity or disorder. In view of this, it is striking that in each successive survey about a quarter of all residents were found to be free of any substantial incapacities, physical or mental. This reflects the continuing demand for residential places for elderly persons mainly for social reasons.

Table 5-1 *Trends in mental infirmity of residents 1977-87 as reported by heads of homes (percentages)*

Resident Characteristics	1977	1979	1981	1983	1985	1987
Severely mentally infirm	9.4	12.3	12.0	12.1	13.9	16.7
Multiple incapacity (mental and up to three forms of physical)	27.8	37.3	37.7	37.4	35.9	40.3
'Normal' mental state	43.5	33.9	31.7	34.2	36.1	31.2
Free of any substantial incapacities	25.2	23.2	21.7	21.4	24.4	24.3

Source: Durham SSD Biennial Day Census of Residents of Homes for the Elderly. D & FP Technical Report No. 87/41 (1987).

The second row of Table 5-1 reports the trend in the proportion of residents who are at least moderately mentally infirm and who also suffer from (i) incapacities affecting their mobility, (ii) an inability to undertake routine self care tasks such as dressing and using the lavatory, and (iii) loss of vision. Table 5-1 shows that it is this and the severely impaired that are the fastest growing groups.

An alternative view of residents' characteristics is presented in Table 5-2. The classification used was devised in conjunction with heads of homes, and the results were obtained from a questionnaire that they each completed. They found the task of classifying the resident mix a complex one. The introduction of the dimension of residents' manageability reflects the often observed contrast between so called 'pleasantly confused' old people and those whose behaviour is disturbed and often disruptive of the communal life of a home. Sometimes mental illness or lifelong psychological characteristics underlie the latter symptoms.

Table 5-2 *Salient characteristics of residents as reported by heads of homes: December 1986 (percentages)*

Mentally lucid including management problems	38
Mildly confused without management problems	15
Very confused without management problems	15
Confused (all degrees) without management problems	18
Psychiatric problems	11
Mentally handicapped	4
Other	Under 1

Two further kinds of evidence about the residents were gathered. First, an analysis of residents' characteristics (including five mental state items of the Modified Crichton Royal Scale) found that the classification of 'severe' mental infirmity was a good predictor of disruptive behaviour. As Table 5-3 indicates, reports of such behaviour are far more commonly ascribed to severely mentally infirm residents than to the remainder. The absolute numbers of problematic residents is often higher for the severely mentally infirm than for the remainder, despite the former constituting only one sixth of the total. This contrast is most conspicuous in the case of frequent wandering and extreme unco-operativeness.

Secondly, a separate analysis of the 27 per cent who were defined as disruptive, revealed that members of this group were far more likely to need extensive help with routine activities than were the remaining residents. Those who were reported to wander frequently, to be persistently restless, or to be generally unco-operative, were found to

Table 5-3 *Contrast between behavioural characteristics of severely mentally infirm residents and remainder, 1987 (percentages)*

	Severe	Remainder
Disruptiveness	74.6	17.3
Frequent wandering	41.5	6.1
Restlessness (all degrees)	48.5	8.5
Unco-operativeness ('totally withdrawn' or 'rejects help')	23.5	2.1

Data Source: Biennial Day Census of Residents, 1987

constitute the majority of the homes' residents with other characteristics, notably incontinence, immobility and an inability to feed, to use the lavatory or to dress, making them more reliant upon staff assistance.

Whereas any increase in the average degree of frailty of residents tends to increase the workload of care staff, an increased incidence of mental infirmity does so in a particular way that is possibly uniquely drastic. This is because three distinct kinds of work are required. First is direct physical assistance with tasks such as washing and dressing. In contrast to a person who is physically incapacitated but mentally alert, a mentally infirm person may require more time because he or she is less motivated to get the activity over, and oblivious to the pressure of work experienced by the care staff. Second, is the role of physically safeguarding residents who may wander onto a busy road. Third, is the work of sensitively intervening so as to keep the peace between confused residents and others. This is made difficult by the fact that the confused person may be literally living in the past, and believe, to give two recorded examples, that he or she owns the home, or that a fellow resident is his or her late spouse. Often conflict may be created or worsened by the provocative reactions to symptoms of mental infirmity displayed by fellow residents or visitors to the home.

What makes this work particularly problematic is not merely that there is more of it, or even that it demands completely new skills, but that it is often perceived as not being a legitimate part of residential care provision. Because of the rapidity of change it is easy for longer serving staff, and others associated with the home, such as the general practitioner, to recall times when severe mental infirmity was exceptional. Examples cited which reflected less pressure on staff, were being able to converse intelligently with all residents, and being able to roster a single staff member for night duty in the knowledge that s/he could work undisturbed at tasks such as ironing and laundry.

Whereas some staff considered that residential care had lost a legitimate social role in this process and not gained an alternative, others strongly disagreed. The latter would tend to argue that, in the past, relatively independent people had been thoughtlessly placed in residential care. A particularly interesting example was a head of home who reported that her predecessor had successfully blocked the admission of very frail clients and had preserved a relatively fit set of residents, reminiscent of earlier decades, up until 1981. This respondent considered that this kind of continuity represented a waste of resources. This indicates a lack of consensus among staff, as to the true role of local authority residential care.

Continuity: established ways of providing care

It can be argued that the major constraint upon providing a satisfactory environment for residents in homes is largely associated with continuity. In other words, the long-standing characteristics of the residential care system have obstructed adjustments to the growing presence of mental infirmity. Continuity has created tight constraints on the possibility of achieving appropriate adjustments to resident mix. This is not to deny the effects of a lack of resources, but rather to assert that the redeployment of available resources is seriously restricted, thereby preserving the service delivery pattern of earlier decades. These areas of continuity and the associated constraining factors are listed in Table 5-4. This continuity is expressed in four main ways: layout, staffing, regime and procedures.

Table 5-4 *Areas of continuity in residential service delivery*

HOME LAYOUTS	Centralised communal amenities
	Lack of privacy
	Prohibitive walking distances
	Lack of enclosed outdoor spaces
	Lack of activity spaces, workshops, day centre
	Extensive bedroom sharing
STAFFING	Low staffing level
	Lack of volunteers
	No clerical support
	No nursing staff
REGIME	Legacy of 'hotel model'
	Few therapeutic interventions
PROCEDURES	Lack of recognition of mental infirmity
	Obsolete admission criteria
	Social Services autarchy
	Variable links with health services

Home layout

The homes studied were originally intended to offer a form of communal living. The idea of these buildings being of high quality was conceived largely in terms of their physical finish, and of the contrast that this presented to that of the Public Assistance institutions they replaced. The resulting design characteristics listed in Table 5-4 constrain adjustment to the current resident mix in three main ways.

First the lack of privacy leads to enforced interaction between confused and other residents. Residents lack the kind of well defined and readily defended personal space which, for instance, single bedsitting rooms that are lockable from the inside would provide. Second, the centralisation of amenities means not only that frail and disorientated residents must walk considerable distances, often with staff assistance, but also that when they reach their destinations their dining or, sometimes, toileting must be done in the presence of others. As a result, daily routines become both tiring and undignified. For instance, residents often dine in the presence of other residents who eat in a messy and invasive manner.

The third way in which constraint is imposed by the layout of the homes is the lack of indoor and outdoor areas in which confused residents can wander in safety. Long dead-end corridors and the general lack of enclosed gardens mean that they can quickly encounter difficulties. If indoors, they are likely to invade the bedrooms of other residents and, if outdoors, there is nothing other than staff vigilance to prevent them wandering onto busy roads. Only the design of the three homes that have been opened since 1982 reflect these considerations.

Staffing

The staffing level is not formally linked to the dependency characteristics of residents, although several formulae having been published over the years (e.g. London Borough of Wandsworth, 1979; Association of Directors of Social Services, 1981). Because staff have to devote a high proportion of their time to meeting the physical care needs of residents, the tendency to neglect social stimulation is reinforced.

The shortage of staff appears to have aggravated the difficulty of recruiting, training and retaining volunteers. The absence of designated clerical staff in homes is also an important constraint. Records relating to residents have become more complex, partly because of more intensive monitoring and assessment, and partly because medical records such as those relating to medication become more complex as residents become more frail. Reduced staffing and increased problems with residents, however, means that heads of homes have to spend more time working directly with residents than was the case in the past. For example, in the course of research, one head had to interrupt a meeting in order to retrieve a resident who had wandered down the adjacent main road in her nightclothes.

Regime

The philosophy of the post-war Labour Government regarding the design and regime of homes for elderly people reflected an analogy with hotels. At the time, the hotel model was seen as a way of distancing new residential provision from the former workhouses. No provision was made for the social stimulation of residents because it was assumed that this would be inappropriately authoritarian, particularly when offered to people who had had highly structured lives thrust upon them either as employees or as recipients of pre-1945 public assistance.

The hotel model of care has constrained the adjustment of homes to the needs of residents in a number of ways. First, the essential role of care staff has been seen as that of offering personal assistance with routine personal tasks such as dressing and bathing. Second, lounges have become arenas for conflict because many residents, due to physical frailty or confusion, have not been able to relax, as would be the case in ordinary hotel lounges. Finally the hotel model has worked against specific therapeutic interventions which might have improved the morale and compatibility of residents. Indeed the model has made it harder for care staff, residents and relatives to acquire an understanding of the character of the common mental disorders. As a result the potential to contain and even reverse certain conditions has not been realised (Lurie et al, 1987).

Procedures

Existing formal criteria for admission tend not to include mental infirmity.

Indeed they actually debar clients with characteristics which, in current practice, are common indicators for admission: mental infirmity, incontinence and an inability to undertake routine self care tasks (Sinclair et al, 1988).

In the past, having relatively fit residents meant that homes did not rely upon the services of other agencies. Nowadays, there is extensive reliance upon the health service, well illustrated by the importance that heads of homes attach to their ability to send very disturbed residents to hospital. In their view admission for only a few days can avert a disastrous lapse in the functioning of a home. However, formal arrangements to ensure such relief do not usually exist. The variation between Health Districts in their resources and in the closeness of their links with home staff is a significant factor in determining the functioning of the homes.

Outcomes: the interaction of continuity and change

The outcomes discussed here are derived from some of the responses of the heads of homes to the questionnaire survey (see Tables 5.5 and 5.6).

Inappropriately placed residents

This measure of failure identified both residents seen as too independent to require residential care, and those who were viewed as too frail or disturbed. The heads of two thirds of the homes identified residents whom they considered were unsuitably placed. Although some residents were thought to be more appropriate for other sheltered community settings, the majority were seen to need more intensive or specialised help than the homes could offer. In particular, the most frequently mentioned option was placement in a psychogeriatric ward, an increasingly rare resource.

Incidents involving mentally infirm residents

Incidents were defined as problematic interactions between mentally infirm and other residents, or acts disruptive to the home's functioning. Heads of homes were asked to report how frequent and how problematic were the following four kinds of incident:

- nocturnal disruption by a confused resident,

- aggression by a confused resident towards a visitor to the home,

- the effects of a confused resident mistaking a fellow resident's bed or belongings as his or her own, and

- conflict arising from a lucid resident's hostility to a confused resident.

Although such incidents occur from time to time in most homes, there is quite marked variation in the frequency of such incidents. In two thirds they occur at least weekly, and in 44 per cent daily. How tolerable such incidents were perceived to be was also something which varied considerably. Although a quarter of heads of homes described them as something they could cope with fairly easily, 64 per cent described them as either 'tiresome' or 'very problematic'.

Adequacy of staffing

As indicated in Table 5-6, heads of homes were generally dissatisfied with staffing levels. In only three homes (8.3% of the total) were they reported

---

Table 5-5 *Outcome measures: stress on homes as social systems (percentages of all homes)*

Inappropriately placed residents:

Homes containing inappropriately placed residents		67
Most widely-cited preferred placement:		
	Psychogeriatric ward	44

Incidents involving mentally infirm residents:

Frequency:	Daily	44
	At least weekly	33
Seriousness:	Very problematic	14
	Tiresome	50
	Can cope fairly easily	25
	No reply	16

Source: Survey of Heads of Homes December 1986

63

to be satisfactory. In half the homes the staffing level was reported to be incompatible with the preferred care regime, and in a further five homes it was judged to be insufficient even for the provision of the routine physical care of residents. Four tasks were cited by the heads of more than 40 per cent of homes as being problematic. The two most widely cited are peculiar to mentally infirm residents, incontinence rarely occurring for purely physical reasons.

Table 5-6 *Further outcome measures (percentages of all homes)*

```
Perceived adequacy of staffing:
    Very satisfactory                               8
    Adequate: further staff would be valuable      17
    Inadequate for preferred care regime           50
    Inadequate for basic physical care             14
    Other                                           8

Most problematic care tasks:
    Orientation of confused residents              56
    Toileting incontinent residents               50
    Toileting physically handicapped residents     47
    Terminal care                                  42
```

Table 5-7 presents a provisional taxonomy of the responses of residents and staff to changes in the mix of residents. These reflect both the potentially stressful circumstances that can arise and the increasingly inappropriate pattern of provision. The preventive measures taken by staff are taken without the support of a clear central policy statement. This means that a specific kind of adaptive measure may be interpreted in different ways in individual homes and, as a result, there is no open pooling of experience (Hunter et al, 1988).

A good example is the creation of 'frail lounges' (Murdoch, 1986). In most homes there are several lounges and thus it is possible to make such designations. Although frowned upon by senior managers, their existence can be interpreted in a number of ways:

■ they are unavoidable given low staffing levels,

■ they reflect practice that is avoidable and bad: frail lounges stigmatise residents and prevent potentially beneficial interaction between mildly confused and lucid residents,

- they enforce rather than prevent interaction between all highly dependent residents: those who are lucid and chairbound as well as those who are mentally infirm and need frequent toileting,

- they provide a low degree of segregation, which creates a location for effective therapeutic work with mentally infirm residents,

- they formalise informal arrangements through which residents themselves impose a pattern of daytime segregation.

Table 5-7   *Adjustments to changed resident mix*

```
By staff:
   Prevention of crises,     e.g. frail lounges,
                                  split sittings for meals,
                                  education of residents,
   Reaction to crises by handling incidents as they happen,

                             e.g. invasion of territory,
                                  wandering onto main road,
   Shift from prevention to reaction to cope with time
   shortage,
                             e.g. by ending toileting routines.

By residents:
   Ignore, befriend, endure or abuse confused residents,
   Resist changes in functioning of home,
                             e.g. transfer of lucid residents
                                  from the largest lounge,
   Seek niche for lucid residents,
                             e.g. in male smokers' lounge.
```

In one home, staff endeavoured to adapt to a changed mix through the education of residents. They asked lucid residents not to be unsympathetic to those who are mentally infirm, and to understand that they now lived in a communal setting and that this meant that they were not entitled to the same assurance of privacy and selection of companions that they may have enjoyed in a private household.

In other cases, a fire brigade approach was used. This meant

65

responding to stressful incidents rather than working to reduce the risk of their occurrence. A disturbing example of this shift from preventive to reactive coping techniques was the ending of toileting programmes. Because of the changing ratio of incontinent residents to care staff, responses to incontinence have been towards 'cleaning up' rather than prevention.

Mentally lucid residents were found to vary considerably in their responses to changes in their environment. Some maintained friendly and even protective relationships with mentally infirm residents, whereas others developed strong and even violent hostility. In one home, a group of women residents tried to resist the proposal of the head of the home to transfer them from the largest lounge, so that this could be used by the growing number of mentally infirm residents.

Conclusions

This research highlights a number of topical and as yet unresolved issues of general interest. One is the aim of securing *optimal* provision for elderly people who are mentally infirm. A second is identifying the most appropriate means of regulating the quality of care of supported clients when Social Services Departments assume their lead role in April 1991.

A series of problems have arisen as relatively long established homes attempt to adjust to changes in their resident mix. One school of thought is that these difficulties are largely attributable to avoidable bad practice. This is exemplified by Potter and Wiseman (1989), and is reflected in recent reports of the Social Services Inspectorate. Culpably bad practice has to be exposed and there is a strong case for fostering consumer empowerment. However, it can be argued that the reality of residential care is often more complex than these prescriptions imply. A distinction can properly be drawn between negligent and insensitive treatment and short cut measures which represent a demonstrable departure from best practice. Examples of the latter have been identified in this research and, as the case of 'frail lounges' illustrates, it is by no means clear whether such adaptations merit praise or criticism, or whether they fall into the category of 'cruel necessity'. What is clear is that policy guidance on such matters is urgently needed.

A second school of thought is that it is sufficient, as well as simply highly desirable, to argue that far more resources should be made available. Increases in inputs, and in particular staffing, would ensure that residential care functioned in the manner intended by national policies.

There is much virtue in both lines of argument in that they are both concerned with alleviating the institutional character of life in homes and the indignities suffered by residents, whether due to understaffing or to poor practice. However, both viewpoints tend to push aside the urgent practical question of how mentally infirm residents, nowadays probably a majority of all residents in local authority residential care, can best be served in a communal setting given current circumstances.

On the question of integration or segregation there is a growing awareness that mental infirmity is increasingly an entry requirement to 'well targeted' local authority residential care. Despite this, the decision about whether to integrate or segregate such residents has been neglected. The most promising policy options are not only highly specific to context, but are able to draw upon an extensive if scattered literature (Coles, 1990). In the first place, it is unconstructive to pose the question in terms of a stark choice between full integration and complete segregation. The range of degrees of mental infirmity is vast. At one extreme is the resident towards whom other residents will feel protective. At the other is the resident who has lost all sexual inhibitions. Some residents are beyond the capacity of any ordinary home and gain nothing from the forms of care that are offered.

There are circumstances, however, in which integrating people with a specific degree of mental infirmity with lucid residents can be therapeutic. Because of this vast diversity of infirmity, it is quite consistent to both promote integration and insist that there must be specialist provision for more severely infirm people. Specialist homes for the severely mentally infirm can be justified on the grounds that this helps to ensure the success of a policy of integration in other residential homes.

Discussion of this kind is specific to homes which require the routine gathering of residents into communal day rooms. It can be argued that because current thinking on the design of homes tends to remove the need for involuntary mixing of this kind, for example by providing lockable service flatlets, then future interest in the issue will diminish. On the contrary, Social Service Departments are to assume new duties of limiting residential care in all sectors to 'high dependency' clients, and to providing an enhanced home registration and inspection service. As a result, the demand for explicit and detailed guidance will greatly increase. In particular, owners of existing private homes who, as a result of the current national policy of 'perverse incentives', have tended to admit relatively fit people, may well find that they must begin to accept mentally infirm people, or quit the business. Although Social Services Departments are likely to be monopoly buyers, they are also likely to be under intense pressure to find relatively cheap residential places for highly dependent clients. Thus once again they may face the difficult task of reconciling residents' needs and providing care in relatively ill-adapted and under-resourced homes, a task which they have hitherto had to tackle only in relation to their own directly managed homes.

6 A survey of the delayed discharge of elderly people from hospitals in an inner city health district

Christina R. Victor

People aged 65 or over are the main consumer group for services provided by the hospitals in the UK. In 1985, 43 per cent of all acute beds were used by people aged 65 or over, compared with 34 per cent in 1965 (OPCS, 1987). They are not confined solely to the specialty of geriatric medicine. They are also the main client group in the specialties of general medicine (44%), general surgery (32%), orthopaedics (27%) and ophthalmology (52%) (OPCS, 1987).

The hospital admission rate increases significantly with age from 185 per 1,000 for those aged 65-74, to 430 per 1,000 for the 85 and over age group (OPCS, 1987). Demographic projections which forecast a 67 per cent increase in the number of people aged 85 and over by the year 2001, have profound implications for the hospital sector of the National Health Service, especially given that average length of hospital stay increases with age. Thus the average length of stay for the 65-74 age group in 1985 was

14.4 days compared with 33.8 for those aged 85 or over (OPCS, 1987). These figures imply that the average person aged 65-74 spends 2.7 days in hospital per year whereas the average person aged 85 or over spends 14.5 days, a five fold increase.

The most appropriate way of providing health care for older people within the hospital sector remains a point of contention. There are protagonists for (Horrocks, 1982) and against (Evans, 1983) the establishment of age-related specialist services for elderly people. Although the merits of each approach have been described, no rigorous evaluation of their effectiveness has been undertaken. However, even if an age-related service is established for those older people with acute medical problems, it seems likely that older people will remain high consumers of services provided in surgery and other specialist areas of modern medicine.

Alongside the debates about the most appropriate method of caring for older patients, are concerns about the 'blocking' of acute beds by older people who no longer need the facilities provided by an acute setting but who, for other reasons, cannot be discharged. It is commonly asserted by clinicians that substantial numbers of acute hospital beds are occupied by older people who no longer need them.

As part of a wider study of the use of hospital facilities within one inner London health district, this paper examines the subject of the blocking of acute beds by elderly people.

The study area

The study was carried out in Paddington and North Kensington (PNK) Health Authority, which has recently merged with Brent Health Authority to form Parkside Health Authority. PNK had a population of approximately 125,000, of whom 13 per cent were aged 65 or over. The district covers an area of approximately four and a half square miles and is one of the most deprived health districts in the country. Compared with national data, older people in PNK are more likely to live alone, reside in private rented housing and experience lower standards of housing (Table 6-1). Levels of community service provision, such as home helps and meals on wheels, approximate to national levels of provision but are considerably below those characteristic of inner London.

Table 6-1 *Characteristics of the population of people of pensionable age in the Paddington and North Kensington area*

	PNK	Great Britain
% living alone	53	34
% female	61	60
% without fixed bath or inside WC	10	5
% housing rented from private landlord	33	12
% aged 85 or more	6	5.5

At the time of the study, PNK was served by two hospitals providing a district general hospital function: St Mary's and St Charles'. No specialist services for the elderly are provided at St Mary's but at St Charles' there are sixty beds designated for acute elderly patients and, in addition, twenty-five long-stay beds provided on the adjacent site.

Method

A census of surgical, medical and acute care was undertaken in May 1988 to identify the number of elderly patients (i.e. aged 65 or over) who were described as being inappropriately placed in an acute bed because they could not be discharged. It was felt that this methodology would highlight the magnitude of perceptions of this problem in the use of hospital beds by elderly people. Although these data are limited through being focused exclusively on elderly people and upon prevalence at a single point in time, previous research has also adopted this approach. Thus, by using this methodology, the results could be compared with other studies.

Medical students visited each ward in the two hospitals studied and identified patients 65 or over who were occupying beds. Medical and/or nursing staff were asked to identify patients who they considered to be 'a delayed discharge', and therefore inappropriately placed on an acute unit on the grounds that they no longer needed the facilities provided. They were then asked to say why such patients could not be discharged or transferred to a more appropriate location. Standard background demographic data such as age, sex and household status, as well as

71

diagnosis and date of admission, were collected from the medical or nursing notes. The patient's use of services before admission, and subsequent referrals to other agencies were also noted.

The patients surveyed

Table 6-2 shows that the census identified a total of 563 patients of whom 287 (51%) were aged 65 or over. The proportion of elderly patients was slightly lower in medicine than in surgery in St. Mary's. In both specialties, people aged 65 or over formed a higher proportion of patients at St Mary's than at St Charles'.

Table 6-2 *Percentage of patients aged 65 or over by specialty and unit*

| | St Mary's | | St Charles' | | | |
	Surgery	Medicine	Surgery	Medicine	Elderly	Total
Percentage aged 65 or over	54	47	32	32	100	51
Total (=100%)	140	137	115	90	81	563

Table 6-3 describes the demographic characteristics of the elderly patients. Overall 59 per cent were female, being concentrated in the medical and care of the elderly wards. The age of patients enumerated ranged from 65 to 98 years, and half of those aged 85 or over were women on the elderly ward at St. Charles'. Table 6-4 shows that the average age of women in each specialty was at least two years older than their male counterparts. Thus, on average, male surgical patients at St Mary's were aged 73 years compared with 76 years for women. Consistently, patients seen at St Mary's were younger than those at St Charles'. Amongst surgical patients, for example, the average age for men was 73 at St Mary's and 77 at St Charles'.

Table 6-5 describes the length of stay in hospital of the elderly patients included in the census. Three main features are evident: female patients have a longer stay than males; surgical patients have the shorter length of

72

Table 6-3 *Demographic characteristics of elderly patients by specialty and unit*

	St Mary's Surgery	Medicine	St Charles' Surgery	Medicine	Elderly	Total
Men						
65–74	17	17	4	9	5	52
75–84	15	11	8	5	19	58
85+	0	3	0	1	3	7
NK	0	0	0	0	0	0
Female						
65–74	14	13	7	1	7	42
75–84	25	16	14	9	23	76
85+	4	4	4	4	23	39
NK	0	1	0	0	1	2
Total	75	65	37	29	81	287

Table 6-4 *Average age of patients aged 65 or over by sex, specialty and unit (years)*

	St Mary's Surgery	Medicine	St Charles' Surgery	Medicine	Elderly
Male	73	74	77	75	79
Female	76	77	79	80	82

Table 6-5 *Average length of stay in days by sex, specialty and unit*

	St Mary's Surgery	Medicine	St Charles' Surgery	Medicine	Elderly
Male	12	20	17	30	80
Female	12	26	20	60	120

stay; and patients treated at St Charles' have a longer average stay than comparable patients at St Mary's.

Delayed discharge and bed blocking

Initially, the definition of 'delayed discharge' was ascribed to those patients who, in the opinion of either a nurse or a doctor, no longer needed all the facilities of an acute unit and were inappropriately placed. Table 6-6 indicates the numbers so judged. Using this definition, it is evident that 24 per cent of all elderly patients were classed as delayed discharges. There were very few such patients on the surgical wards. However, 28 per cent of medical patients and 43 per cent of acute elderly patients were considered by staff to be inappropriately placed. Patients at St Charles' were consistently more likely to be considered to be inappropriately placed than their equivalents at St Mary's. However, as already noted, patients at St. Charles' were, on average, older than those at St. Mary's.

Table 6-6 *Percentages of patients defined by staff as inappropriately placed, by specialty and unit*

| | St Mary's | | St Charles' | | | |
	Surgery	Medicine	Surgery	Medicine	Elderly	Total
Percentage inapprop. placed	7	23	11	34	43	24
Total	75	65	37	29	81	287

Simply asking staff to identify inappropriately placed patients is, however, potentially subject to bias from several sources. To allow for this, doctors' and nurses' opinions on the identity of inappropriately placed patients were investigated by cross-tabulating their separate responses to the same question (Table 6-7). This shows a good degree of agreement when both medical and nursing staff were interviewed. However, interpretation of the table is limited because the small number of interviews undertaken with medical staff meant that only two-thirds of the patients were assessed by doctors.

Table 6-7 *Comparison of nurses' and doctors' assessment of appropriateness of placement*

Doctor's opinion	Nurse's opinion appropriate	inappropriate	not known	Total
appropriate	40	2	0	42
inappropriate	2	145	0	147
not known	24	74	0	98
Total	66	221	0	287

Some previous research, which has considered the problem of the blocking of acute beds, has related this to length of stay rather than to the views of staff. Thus, to facilitate comparisons, 'delayed discharges' or 'blockers' were re-defined as those with a minimum length of stay of four weeks *and* who, in the opinion of either medical or nursing staff, no longer needed the facilities of an acute unit. On this basis, length of stay is cross-tabulated in Table 6-8 against whether the patient was considered to be inappropriately located.

Table 6-8 *Assessment of appropriateness of placement by length of stay*

Length of stay	inapprop.	approp.	Total
Less than 4 weeks	25	181	206
4 weeks or more	43	38	81
Total	68	219	287

Of patients in the census, 28 per cent (81) had been in hospital for four weeks or more and nearly a half of these patients (38) were rated as appropriately located. The rest (43) were rated as inappropriately located and could, therefore, be defined as 'delayed discharges' or 'bed blockers'. These forty-three patients were occupying 8 per cent of the 563 beds that were covered by the census.

Three groups of patients are now distinguished: the 43 blockers, the 38 other long-stay patients, and the 206 short-stay patients. Table 6-9 shows that the majority of bed blockers and long-stay patients were located on the acute geriatric ward at St. Charles'. There were also more blockers on the medical ward at St. Charles'.

Table 6-9   *Patient classification by specialty and unit (percentages)*

	St Mary's Surgery	Medicine	St Charles' Surgery	Medicine	Elderly	Total number
Blockers	5	6	0	28	33	43
Long-stay	8	9	8	7	26	38
Short-stay	87	85	92	66	41	206
Total (=100%)	75	65	37	29	81	287

Table 6-10 compares the characteristics of the three groups. There were no significant differences on age, sex and living alone. However, it is evident that the bed blockers were more likely to be demented, incontinent and to have had an admission in the previous six months. In contrast, the highest rates of immobility and the lowest rates of emergency admissions were found in the long-stay group. Furthermore, the long-stay patient group had the highest average age.

Table 6-10   *Characteristics of patients by group*

	Blockers	Long-stay	Short-stay
average age	79	80	76
% female	62	64	51
% living alone	60	68	56
% emergency admission	70	57	77
% incontinent	53	32	17
% demented	50	21	10
% immobile	42	71	12
% admission in previous six months	20	5	10
Total	43	28	206

Other services

Table 6-11 describes the receipt of community care services by the three groups in the month before admission. Rates of service use were significantly higher among the bed blockers than the other two groups. However, it is important to note that by no means all the patients in this group had been receiving the full support of the community services.

Table 6-11 *Percentage receiving services in month before admission by group*

	Blockers	Long-stay	Short-stay
District nurse	42	16	8
Home help	35	16	15
Meals	19	8	6
Total (= 100%)	43	38	206

The referral of patients to other services whilst in hospital are shown in Table 6-12. It is evident that long-stay and bed-blocking patients are more likely to be referred to therapeutic services than short-stay patients. However, it is worth noting that the remedial/rehabilitative services are not involved with the majority of elderly people admitted to hospital.

Table 6-12 *Referral to services*

	Blockers	Long-stay	Short-stay
Geriatrician/ Psychogeriatrician	70	53	17
Occupational therapist	44	42	7
Physiotherapy	56	53	13
Social work	56	55	8
Total (= 100%)	43	38	206

Table 6-13 describes the reasons given for the forty-three blocking patients being assessed to be inappropriately placed. Overall, the single most frequently cited reason was the need for nursing home care (21 out of 43). Amongst medical and surgical patients, the most important reason given for blockers being inappropriately placed was the need for geriatric care or assessment.

Table 6-13 *Reasons for 'blockers' being defined as inappropriately placed, by specialty*

	Surgical	Medical	Elderly	Total
Needs psychiatric care	0	0	4	4
Needs rehabilitation	1	1	1	3
Needs nursing home care	0	5	16	21
Needs long-term care	0	0	5	5
Needs geriatric care	3	6	0	9
Has social problems	0	0	0	0
Needs community care	0	0	1	1
Total	4	12	27	43

Discussion

A survey of all acute beds in a London health authority was undertaken to establish the number of beds 'blocked' by elderly patients. On the day the census was undertaken, 51 per cent of all acute beds in the specialties of geriatric medicine, medicine and surgery were occupied by people aged 65 or over.

The generally accepted definition of a 'bed blocker' was used in this study: a patient who has been in hospital for more than four weeks *and* who, in the opinion of medical or nursing staff, no longer requires the facilities provided in an acute setting. It is worth emphasising that the blocking of beds by inappropriately placed patients is not a feature unique to elderly people.

Using this definition, the survey revealed that 8 per cent of acute beds were considered to be blocked by elderly patients. This proportion is more than the 4.8 per cent reported by Rubin and Davies (1975) in Liverpool, but less than the 14 per cent described by Coid and Crome (1986) in Bromley. If the comparison is limited to people aged 65 years or over, then the proportion described as bed blockers is 15 per cent which is very similar to the 17 per cent reported by Coid and Crome. However, it remains substantially higher than the 9 per cent reported by Rubin and Davies, probably because these authors surveyed all patients aged 60 years or over.

The distribution of bed blockers varied between medical specialties. Like the study of Seymour and Pringle (1982), this survey identified comparatively few elderly bed blockers in surgical wards. Similar findings were reported by Coid and Crome (1986). Several reasons may account for why so few surgical patients are defined as bed blockers. First the younger age of patients treated on surgical wards could mean that this patient group is less likely to present the multiplicity of problems which tend to characterise the bed-blocking elderly patient. Alternatively, it could be that surgeons are able to discharge patients or transfer them elsewhere before they become problems.

It was evident that not all elderly people who had been in hospital for more than four weeks were defined as inappropriately placed. Consequently, a threefold typology of patients was developed, following Coid and Crome (1986). In contrast to their study, where the bed blockers were significantly older than long-stay or other patient groups, there was no statistically significant difference in the age of the three groups. However, like their study, the blocking group were more likely to have problems such as incontinence and dementia which are likely to present considerable demands upon nursing care.

The rates of service use before admission were substantially higher amongst the blocking group than is characteristic of elderly people living in the community. In PNK, approximately 8 per cent of those aged 65 or over receive a home help compared with 35 per cent of bed blockers. However, the receipt of support services had not been universal. Furthermore, the present study revealed that only half the long-stay and bed-blocking groups had subsequently been referred to rehabilitation services. Thus a substantial proportion of elderly patients are not being referred to these services even after they have been classed as bed blockers. The majority of those patients who were not referred were located on the surgical and medical wards. This would seem to support the work of Victor and Vetter (1985) who reported that patients treated on geriatric wards were more likely to be referred to services than their counterparts treated in general medicine.

The majority of elderly people who were defined as bed blockers (81%) were considered to require some form of long-term institutional care. This is rather more than the 60 per cent of blockers in the Bromley survey who were awaiting long-term care. This variation in the proportion requiring institutional care may reflect the paucity of domiciliary services in Paddington and North Kensington, and the high proportion of elderly people living alone. However, it is disappointing to find that hospital staff were so willing to think that institutional care was the most appropriate means of caring for these elderly patients, when several studies have documented how frail elderly people can be successfully maintained in the community.

It is commonly asserted that there are large numbers of elderly people occupying acute beds who cannot be discharged because of their inappropriate social circumstances. Indeed it was expected that a substantial proportion of elderly patients in this survey would fall into this category because of the proven poor housing and low levels of social support in this part of London. However, few such patients were identified. This could reflect the timing of the census and, had the study been undertaken in the winter months, the proportion in this category might have been greater. Nevertheless, the study does suggest that the misuse of hospital services may be commonly exaggerated.

Acknowledgements

The Community Medicine and Nursing Research Unit gratefully acknowledges the financial support of Parkside Health Authority and the Special Trustees of St Mary's Hospital. The help of the medical students who collected the data during their Community Medicine project work is also gratefully acknowledged.

7 Evolutionary lessons for the future of day care, or where do we go from here?

Michael R. Nolan

Tibbitt (1987) notes that the provision of day care on all fronts has been a key feature of health and social services policy in recent years and that this has resulted in a rapid expansion and diversification, nowhere more apparent than in the field of day care for the elderly. These developments have occurred in concert with the drive for community care, in which day services form one of the main avenues of support (Fennell et al, 1981, Cantley and Smith, 1987). Thus day care continues to be described in glowing terms in policy statements (Welsh Office, 1985) despite the fact that there is little objective evidence for its effectiveness, a phenomenon termed the 'reborn certainty' (McCoy, 1983).

This chapter contends that rigid demarcations between the various agencies providing day care for the elderly have resulted in a service which manifestly fails to address the needs of an increasingly large dependent section of the elderly population and their carers. It is suggested that the basis for such a failure is rooted in the struggle for professional recognition and prestige, particularly in the field of geriatric medicine.

Consequently, as Carter (1981) noted, those most in need of day care are those least able to get it. The development of day care for the elderly, and more particularly the day hospital, is described alongside the growth of geriatric medicine as a specialist service, and the current dichotomised position of the day hospital is highlighted by reference to research conducted by the author in North Wales (Nolan, 1986). The disruptive effects of present organisational practices on the dependent elderly and their carers are considered, and suggestions made as to how day care might evolve in order to better meet their needs.

The development of geriatric medicine

A brief description, attempted in a few lines, cannot possibly do justice to the undoubted benefits that have accrued to the elderly as a result of the development of geriatric medicine. After the therapeutic nihilism of the 1930s, the pioneering efforts of Marjorie Warren pulled the practice of medicine with the elderly up by its very boot straps. However, as Wilkin and Hughes (1986) note, such a metamorphosis has not been achieved without opposition, most notably from other medical specialties. The cornerstone of modern geriatric medicine lies in the premise that the conditions of old age are treatable (Millard, 1988). However, many such conditions are not curable in the best traditions of the medical model. Faced with this dilemma and the threat it poses to the credibility of geriatric medicine in the eyes of its more prestigious peers, the primacy of cure has been replaced by rehabilitation and a functional model of health was substituted for the medical model (Wilkin and Hughes, 1986). The result is progressive patient care, accompanied by the proud and defiant assertion that geriatric medicine, more than any other specialty, comes closest to the Alma Ata declaration, being concerned as it is with the clinical, rehabilitative, social and preventive aspects of illness and health in the elderly (Hall, 1988).

Yet, despite or perhaps because of this assertion, continued dependency is seen as a failure of progressive patient care and discharge remains the ultimate goal. Service developments do all they can to expedite this aim (Hall, 1988). Within such a paradigm, chronic disease and disability occupy an uncertain and ambiguous position. As the demography of the industrialised world changes with the rise in the numbers of those aged 85 or over and the concomitant increase in disability, the supremacy of the medical approach to health is threatened. Moreover, it is becoming ever less defensible in terms of efficiency, economics or ethics (Allan and Hall, 1988).

Concurrently, the debate as to the value of maintaining geriatric medicine as a distinct specialty has resurfaced with renewed vigour. Once again therefore, geriatric medicine is a beleaguered ship, and the battle cry is sounded with the call to reach towards 'new horizons' (Millard, 1988). However, upon examination, the 'horizons' envisaged are certainly not new in the sense of being original and appear to be merely an attempt to reinforce the traditional power base of consultant medical staff. Viewed against this historical backcloth and given the siege mentality it has engendered, it is easy to appreciate how the breadth of vision which characterised the birth of the day hospital has been replaced by its present inward looking stance.

The evolution of the day hospital

Hildick-Smith (1977) traces the origins of the day hospital to the psychiatric services of pre-war Russia from whence it spread, firstly to Montreal and New York, reaching Britain in the late 1940s. The application of day care to the field of geriatric medicine began in the 1950s through the work of early advocates such as Cosin (1954) and Droller (1958). At this stage the geriatric day hospital had broadly based aims. The value of supporting the carer and of improving, through social contact, the mental outlook of the chronic sick was recognised. In addition, the day hospital had more overtly therapeutic and instrumental functions: saving hospital beds, facilitating discharge, and allowing continued treatment, investigation and rehabilitation (Ministry of Health, 1957). However, the hostile environment within which geriatric medicine strove for recognition required that the fledgling service demonstrate a treatment orientated approach. Therefore, from the early 1960s onwards, the aims of the day hospital evolved accordingly. In 1964, Brocklehurst described it has having a predominantly medical regime in which discharge became the fundamental goal, and the treatment of loneliness and depression, hitherto a legitimate function for the day hospital, was ascribed to the day centre. The difficulties in discharging the heavily dependent elderly became apparent at a similarly early stage (Woodford-Williams and Alvarez, 1964), and geriatricians attributed this failure to a lack of day centre places. By 1970, a clear distinction, at least in the minds of geriatricians, had been drawn between the day hospital and the day centre. It was considered that the day centre should accommodate the disabled elderly in order that the day hospital fulfil its discharge criteria (Andrews et al, 1970). This trend culminated in 1971 in a government statement of day hospital function.

> Day hospital functions are rehabilitation of the elderly who may have been ill, and by active treatment and supervision maintaining independence when threatened. It may also be useful for the assessment of patients who do not need to be admitted for this purpose,but who cannot be adequately assessed at home or at an out-patient consultation. (Department of Health and Social Security, 1971).

Any legitimate role for the day hospital in the relief of carers or in improving the mental outlook of the chronic sick, had now lost its official sanction and the supposedly symbiotic relationship between the day hospital and the day centre had gained further significance. However, the day centre had less clearly articulated aims (Greenfield, 1974), and the resulting confusion regarding day care in general has been described by a number of commentators (Morley, 1974; Bowl et al, 1978; Clegg, 1978; Fennell et al, 1981). What is clear is that the sharp demarcation lines that geriatricians sought to establish do not extend to policy makers in other disciplines. According to Fennell et al (1981), 'the notion of the day centre as having important relationships to the day hospital is so far removed from their thinking that it does not occur to them even to raise it'. Furthermore, even where there are sufficient day centre places, the number of individuals who successfully transfer from one to the other is small, and this may be because the day centre represents a less personally and socially acceptable alternative (Wagstaff, 1979).

Despite these anomalies, geriatricians still attribute the failure of the day hospital to discharge its long stay attenders to a lack of day centre places and they cling to discharge as a measure of its success. The functioning of the day hospital is therefore strongly influenced by the perceptions of a few prominent geriatricians whose pronouncements are used to assess the attitudes of other staff members (Carter, 1981). The gatekeeper role of the geriatricians reinforces their pivotal position and ensures that eligibility criteria are enforced in determining admission to the day hospital.

It is abundantly clear, however, that the perceptions of geriatricians are at variance with those of most other groups. Many day hospital staff, particularly nursing and occupational therapists, would prefer it had a wider role (Brocklehurst and Tucker, 1980; Carter, 1981). Additionally, general practitioners, as the main referral agents, have differing views. Hildick-Smith (1981) and Thompson (1974) consider that general practitioners require education as to the proper function of the day hospital because they attribute equal if not greater importance to its social role in supporting carers as they do to any treatment function. Consequently, general practitioners make a number of 'inappropriate' referrals (Gooch and Luxton, 1977), possibly as Tyndall (1978) has suggested, to relieve their own anxieties rather than to benefit the patient.

The clinical objectives of the day hospital, emphasising discharge, are also at variance with the wishes of many users and their carers (Carter, 1981; Smith et al, 1983; Cantley and Smith, 1987). Discharge has always been known to cause 'considerable disappointment' to many patients (Brocklehurst, 1964), and it is apparent that such decisions are contrary to the real wishes of many attenders, their carers and general practitioners (Hildick-Smith, 1977). There seems to be an awareness that current day hospital services function in a way that is contrary to the wishes of the vast majority of individuals who use them, and yet there remains an insistence on adhering to just such a system:

> Day hospitals should be for treating medical conditions, not providing social support. Nor should they be used for providing relief for relatives of elderly people who are considered too physically or mentally disabled for day centres. (Murphy, 1985).

The maintenance of this distinction between the day hospital and the day centre is said to be beneficial to geriatricians as the non-scientific accoutrements of day care have low status (Wadsworth et al, 1972; Carter, 1981). The overall result, however, is that both the health and the social services are helpless to address the needs of heavily dependent people and can only offer inappropriate solutions (Williams, 1980).

The North Wales study

The precise nature of the difficulties caused to the users of the day hospital system by its current rigid role definition, were explored as part of a wider study of day hospital usage conducted by the author in North Wales (Nolan, 1986). The data are taken from a series of semi-structured interviews with day hospital staff, and with 73 elderly patients, 35 carers and 20 general practitioners. As such, they represent differing perceptions of day hospital functions and of the benefits of attendance.

Day hospitals in the study area were guided by an operational policy that reflected national objectives (Department of Health and Social Security, 1971), and which identified a maximum desirable attendance period of three months. Many day hospital staff considered that such an operational definition had an unnecessarily restrictive effect on day to day practice. Staff, particularly in the more rural units, felt that discharge was inappropriate for many of the more disabled attenders. They considered that attendance to relieve relatives, or to provide continued motivation to the elderly themselves, represented legitimate day hospital functions. Geriatricians were clearly sympathetic to such a view but continued to adhere to a discharge policy in the majority of cases. However, in an effort to accommodate the heavily disabled attender who required a degree of permanency, some units allowed three months rotating attendance, whereas others offered permanent places to such individuals. A comparative study of two units, one operating the former system and one the latter, brought into relief the results of the two differing management strategies for the users and their carers.

Users' views

The characteristics of the study population indicated a heavily dependent group of users with 70 per cent being aged 75 or over, and 64 per cent suffering the effects of either a stroke or arthritis. Their views on the benefits of the day hospital were, however, remarkably consistent.

There was a small group of users, usually younger and more recently diagnosed, who saw the day hospital in purely instrumental terms. Whilst in the main they enjoyed the experience, they had no desire to prolong it longer than was necessary. For the majority of users, however, the day

86

hospital was far more than this and constituted a major part of their coping strategy, with an important part to play in maintaining self esteem and morale.

The concept of therapy was still a very important, albeit diffuse, notion. Whilst many patients could not clearly articulate the nature of the therapy they were receiving, the fact that they had been referred for it, and considered themselves to be getting it, was important and achieved a number of purposes. Firstly, it legitimised their attendance. They were attending for the benefit of their health and not because they could not cope or were a nuisance to their relatives. Secondly, it offered hope, however minimal, for improvement or at least indicated that they had not been entirely written off. The majority of attenders, having suffered from their complaints for some time, were unlikely to make a dramatic functional improvement and were well aware of this. However, the very fact that they were attending the day hospital, belied the fact that they had 'no hope', and such a distinction was important to their morale and perception of themselves as being someone who mattered. In such circumstances hope was not false, but real in the sense defined by Lynch in Rideout (1986) of there being a greater than zero expectation of achieving a particular goal. Thirdly, it allowed many attenders to witness individuals who they considered to be worse off than themselves. It did not matter that, in objective terms, such a perception was erroneous. Even if the perceiver was in fact functionally worse, the perception itself still had the effect of creating a 'what have I got to worry about' philosophy which rationalised the current position and made complaining seem niggardly.

A further important concept was that of reciprocity. Space precludes a full discussion of the nature of reciprocity, but it is increasingly realised that it is an important component of self esteem that has a major part to play in both the social construction of dependency (Wilkin, 1986) and in understanding the basis of informal care (Bulmer, 1987). Day hospital attendance facilitated reciprocity at a number of levels, from the simple production of craft goods offered for sale by the day hospital to abstract notions of assisting those worse off than oneself.

Eastman (1976) has noted that the elderly are constantly confronted with images of themselves as useless and of no worth. Nowhere is this more apparent than in the case of heavily dependent elderly people. The day hospital, by allowing for hope and reciprocity, did much to reverse such images. Charmaz (1983) considers that loss of 'self' is the most fundamental form of suffering in chronic illness, and has described how outwardly superficial social interactions can assume tremendous significance for such individuals. Contact with health personnel are particularly influential, especially those which reinforce feelings of personal worth. Conversely, discrediting contacts with health personnel are all the more destructive. This loss of self can be ameliorated by the preservation of hope, a vital ingredient in adaptation to long term disability (Craig and Edwards, 1983; Rideout, 1986). Hazan (1980) has described in detail how day care attendance allows the disabled elderly person to create a new temporal dimension based on the concept of reciprocal care. Within such a dimension, elderly people are no longer old and useless: each has something to offer to the other. On this basis, it is easy to appreciate how the day hospital has come to occupy such a central position in the lives of dependent elderly people.

It was also apparent from interviews that, in addition to the important psychological benefits of attendance, many individuals also acquired new skills, knowledge or services that were of more direct instrumental benefit. The health advice of the nursing sister was particularly appreciated, many of the respondents not wishing to 'bother' the doctor with common but nonetheless worrying complaints. Similarly, the simple chair exercises taught by the physiotherapist were considered to be very useful and were often reported to be continued at home. For many, these exercises resulted in a functional improvement, but even if they did not they were still clearly important in conveying the idea that there was something they could do that was under their control.

Discharge, on the other hand, negated all the above and was a topic which engendered great unease in many attenders. They described how they dreaded the 'three months out' and would do all they could to delay this. Tactics ranged from bargaining with staff for an extension, to a spurious 'worsening' of their complaint in an attempt to meet the medical eligibility criteria.

Carers' views

From the interviews conducted with the carers, the lasting impression was one of individuals providing care at great personal cost, suffering considerable hardship as a consequence. The burdens that caring imposes are becoming increasingly well documented (Bonny, 1984; Henwood and Wicks, 1984; Parker, 1985), and the need to provide appropriate support to this group has recently received considerable media attention. It was clear that, for the carers who were interviewed, the day hospital represented a potential lifeline. However, the fact is that any benefits to carers of day hospital attendance are often considered as 'incidental' (Irvine, 1980). This attitude inhibits units in reaching their full potential in this area.

Probably the single most valued benefit to carers was the break that the day hospital provides. This, as one carer put it, allowed a return to some semblance of normality, no matter how brief that period was. As with carers in previous studies (Nissel and Bonnerjea, 1982), this break was not used to relax, at least not in the physical sense, as most carers used the time to carry out routine domestic tasks. On the other hand, it did allow respite from the constant worry that faces carers. They could relax in the knowledge that, at least for a few hours, their dependant was the responsibility of someone else. Early research into the value of day hospitals has questioned the effectiveness of one or two days respite per week (Farndale, 1961). However, for those interviewed this was not in doubt. Whilst some would have liked more frequent attendance, most would have been happy with current arrangements if a degree of permanency could have been relied upon. The rota system, where it was operating, proved extremely disruptive to the routines of carers who could not establish a regular pattern to their care.

In addition to the break, the day hospital also fulfilled a number of other useful purposes. For those carers who had regular contact, the day hospital was a source of advice, information and emotional support. Once again the role of the nursing sister was crucial in this respect. As with the elderly themselves, carers did not like to bother the doctor with apparently mundane worries about the health of their dependant. The sister, on the other hand, was a credible and readily available source of advice whom carers felt less inhibited about approaching, once initial contact had been made with the day hospital. Unfortunately, none of the units in the study area established routine contact with all carers, a finding consistent with the national situation (Brocklehurst and Tucker, 1980; Carter, 1981). Contact was only established where a problem was perceived to exist or where the carer took the initiative. It was apparent from the interviews that carers lacked even rudimentary knowledge about their dependant's condition but were reluctant to admit to their ignorance and approach the day hospital staff. The latter, on the other hand, whilst being most helpful once contact had been made, were reluctant to approach all carers lest this encouraged dependence and inhibited discharge.

Day hospital attendance also provided many carers with the feeling that something was being done to lighten their load, even if this was only on a temporary basis. In this sense it represented, as Muir-Gray (1984) suggests, 'a symbol of the commitment of the health and social services to sharing the care with relatives'. Furthermore, the carers particularly valued the bath their dependant received, and a number considered that the improved psychological state of their dependant made their task easier.

The deleterious effects of rotating discharge have already been touched upon and most of the carers interviewed anticipated this with overt dread. Consultants, general practitioners and carers themselves described how carers would plead for their dependant not to be discharged, and this was something which general practitioners in particular found hard to deal with as, in the majority of cases, they agreed with the carer.

General practitioners' views

The literature previously cited suggested that general practitioners are not aware of day hospital functions and fail to adequately differentiate between the day hospital and day centre. This was certainly not the case in the present study. All twenty general practitioners interviewed were fully aware of the written distinctions between the two services, but the majority felt that such distinctions had little or no validity in the light of the problems they faced. Whilst acknowledging the value of treatment and investigation, the single most important function of the day hospital was described in terms of continued support for dependent elderly people and their carers, again a finding consistent with previous work (Thompson, 1974; Hildick-Smith, 1981; Cantley and Smith, 1987).

However, general practitioners knew how the system functioned and played the game accordingly. The need to supply a legitimate reason for each referral, that is one couched in 'treatment' terms, led to the use of 'catch all' categories which submerged the real need under a legitimising label. While this tactic worked well enough in satisfying day hospital eligibility criteria, it did nothing to ease the real system-created problem of the discharge of patients. Even in areas which had access to day centre places, a viable alternative was not really available, either because of the day centre's own eligibility criteria and limited transport arrangements, or else because the elderly individual concerned refused to attend. General practitioners could not see the relevance of a continued discharge regime when the area of greatest need was being papered over:

> Medicine has a very blinkered approach to the care of the elderly. The application of a curative model is often wholly inappropriate.

> Medicine is too concerned with semantics. What is treatment? It is whatever is effective for that patient.

> The health services deny their responsibility (for the disabled elderly) and hide behind the medical model. The social services disown this group because of their disabilities. A huge gap exists which must be filled.

Rota systems

The problems that the current policy causes for the patients, their carers and general practitioners were exacerbated in units operating a well defined rota system. It should be reiterated at this point that the rota system was a genuine attempt to address the needs of the heavily dependent and their carers in a way that (i) acknowledged their need for continued attendance, and (ii) met the discharge criteria of the day hospital. The system was an undoubted success in the latter objective but usually an abject failure in the former. It also made units operating such a system look more efficient than they were, and those units which accepted permanent attenders look the opposite. Take the following examples:

- Unit A operates a three monthly rota system whereby patients attend for three months twice a week, are then discharged for three months, this system being repeated. In a twelve month period the patient would have attended about fifty times and the records would show four admissions and four discharges, each within the recommended three month period. As a result the impression given is of one hundred per cent success.

- Unit B admits a patient for the entire twelve month period but attendance is only once per week. Over the twelve month period the total number of attendances is about fifty per patient but the records show one admission and no discharges. As a result the impression given is of one hundred per cent failure.

The latter system, even allowing for the reduced weekly attendance, accorded more closely with the wishes of the service users, but it is a clear second best in terms of discharge, the performance indicator that tends to dominate.

Conclusions

According to Horobin (1987), the tension between using day services as a means of providing long-term support or as a stepping stone to independence, is apparent in all forms of day care. He contends that both are valid and needed, but that the trick is getting the balance right. This paper has suggested that the present organisation of day care for elderly people, and more particularly for the highly dependent and their carers, is badly out of balance. What then is the way forward?

Faced with the above scenario, service providers can react in one of two ways (Horobin, 1987). They can respond in a paternalistic fashion and continue to impose their own version of the users 'real' needs, or they can allow users to develop a system which addresses their own perception of their needs. It would seem that the present definition of the day hospital is almost entirely the result of the former approach. Whilst Tibbett (1987) doubts that there is sufficient consensus to provide a clear aim for day care, the expanding literature on the needs of dependent elderly people and their carers can do much to inform the debate.

Day care owes its original expansion to the major support role accorded it in the drive for community care. It is now recognised that the two forms of care most important in maintaining the elderly in the community are self care and informal care (Muir-Gray, 1988), and it is to these two areas that day care should address itself. In order to do so successfully, it must evolve from its present state to incorporate elements which acknowledge the importance of psycho-social components of health, and which recognise carers to be a legitimate focus for a health related approach. This requires, as Wilkin and Hughes (1986) note, the acceptance of a truly holistic concept of health in which the views of users are not *an* important element but *the* important element.

With the day hospital marginalising the frail elderly and all but excluding their carers, and the day centre largely unable to accommodate this user group, day care for the elderly, as it now exists, cannot hope to achieve its potential. Farndale, writing of the emerging day care service in 1961, suggested that there was a need for experimentation and close co-operation between all the agencies involved in service provision. Such an observation is as pertinent today as it was almost thirty years ago, and yet the intervening period appears to have brought us no closer.

This chapter is entitled 'evolutionary lessons for the future of day care' and evolution is a hard task master, as the dodo might have testified had it learned its lessons in time. Whatever the future of day care for the elderly, some form of creative synthesis is indicated if it is to survive in anything but its present fragmented form. This will require, at the very least, that rigid and inflexible professional definitions of legitimate service function become malleable. Millard (1988), in his call for new horizons in the health care of the elderly, begins his statement with a Chinese proverb: 'A journey of a thousand miles starts with but a single step'. History often turns full circle and it would be a useful first step in the evolution of day care if the day hospital returned to the broadly based definition of its role with which it began.

8 Preparation for retirement in the European Community: intentions and practice

John Lansley, Maggie Pearson and Kathy Pick

In any study of service provision we need to start by asking whether the service is needed at all. Is retirement a problem? Do people need help in preparing for it? The point was made for us when we asked a government researcher in Denmark why, in a country with a high level of retirement pensions, with extensive welfare services for elderly people, and with figures for participation in adult education about ten times as great as those for the United Kingdom, there appeared to be little formal preparation for retirement (PFR). His reply was that, perhaps for these very reasons, Danish people did not see retirement as a problem. They had completed their working lives and were happy now to make way for younger people who needed jobs. They themselves could look forward to a fulfilling and comfortable retirement. If they needed advice on pensions, the Ministry of Social Affairs could provide it. To go on a course on how to retire would suggest that retirement was difficult, and this was an idea which they neither accepted nor wished to accept. While our own study suggests that this picture of the Danish situation needs modifying, this response is useful in posing the questions: what preparation, and why? They may be phrased more specifically: is retirement a problem, and if so for whom? And can people be 'prepared' for it?

Changes in the pattern and understandings of retirement

There is not sufficient space here to consider the different analyses and interpretations of the phenomenon of retirement which have been developed since the war (Atchley, 1976; Phillipson, 1982). We should note, however, that many people still regard retirement as critical or problematic. Some think of it more crudely as being synonymous with old age. Popular perceptions of retirement, although often atheoretic, have inevitably been influenced by theories of ageing. Thus in the 1960s, the conflicting theories of disengagement (Cumming and Henry, 1961) and activity (Friedmann and Havighurst, 1954; Miller, 1965) could be used to interpret retirement differently. On the one hand, it could be seen as the start of the period of old age: retirement could be regarded as a paradigm of the whole process of disengagement, and it followed that preparation for retirement was to do with preparation for old age. Activity theory, on the other hand, interpreted retirement as a point of severe role loss, and this could be used to justify preparation for retirement work as a means of overcoming this (Phillipson and Strang, 1983). Even if we adopt more modern theories, and deploy the concept of the social construction of old age (Phillipson, 1982; Townsend, 1986), there are still dangers that retirement might come to be regarded by some as a time when people are forced into the roles of old age by economic necessity or through social expectations.

Yet these models of retirement bear increasingly little relationship to the actual facts of retirement. To take the most obvious point, retirement ages, both statutory and de facto, have decreased considerably since the war (Laczko et al, 1988). The concept has been developed of a 'third age' of retirement, an age which is quite separate from the stereotyped dependencies of old age. Certainly, the idea has emerged of there being two 'nations' within the retired population of many societies. One nation has considerable resources, of health, wealth and increasing disposable income, and commercial interests have not been slow to identify this potential new market. The other does not have such resources.

Another significant development has been the increased participation of women in the formal labour market. This is something which, from the point of view of retirement preparation, challenges the old myth that women are 'naturally' housewives who never retire. As will be discussed later in this paper, there are specific issues concerning women's retirement which have scarcely been addressed (Szinovacz, 1982).

The significant changes in the pattern of retirement, then, are the changing and growing proportion of retired people, their tendency to retire earlier whether voluntarily or through compulsory redundancy, and the rising number of women in the labour market who are increasingly involved in retirement.

What is the need for preparation for retirement?

The current levels of economic activity in the European Community are shown in Table 8-1. If these tables summarise the main characteristics of the retired people of the European Community, what preparation if any will be of benefit for their retirement? In our view, this should not include preparation for their old age. The challenges normally associated with old age are typically twenty or more years away at retirement. Advice given on such matters in preparing for retirement will be outdated by the time it is needed.

Advice on ageing is taking the form, in practice, not of educational gerontology but of gerontological education (Glendenning, 1986), and retired people are learning about the problems of old age instrumentally, not as regards themselves, but in order to aid them as carers of elderly relatives. In the same way, 40 year olds are joining Ensamme Gamles Vaern (EGV) in Denmark because they see their parents facing the issues of retirement. The need to care for elderly dependants may well become a constraint on the enjoyment of retirement for an increasing number of people. This does not, however, justify advice on the needs and support of old people in general PFR courses. Rather it requires specific provision.

Available evidence suggests that, while over two thirds of people are happy in their retirement (Beck, 1983; Beauchesne, 1985; Holmgaard with Pedersen, 1985; Whelan et al, 1985), satisfaction may be limited by two main factors: health and income. These are, of course, the determinants not only of a happy retirement, but of contentment with any stage of life.

96

Table 8-1 *Male and female participation in the labour market and age points of withdrawal from it (percentages)*

Age	50-54		55-59		60-64		65-69	
	M	F	M	F	M	F	M	F
West Germany	93	50	78	38	33	11	9	3
France	90	56	62	40	25	15	8	4
Italy	90	33	70	20	39	11	15	4
Netherlands	83	29	68	19	30	7	7	(1)
Belgium	85	29	62	17	27	5	6	(2)
Luxembourg	87	28	56	18	(19)	(9)		
United Kingdom	91	65	83	52	55	19	14	6
Ireland	89	28	82	23	65	15	27	(6)
Denmark	90	72	83	58	47	26	28	9
Greece	89	40	76	30	54	21	27	11
Spain*	89		81		59		12	
EC*	90	48	73	35	39	14	13	5

* Figures for Spain are from the 1981 population census. No figures are included in the overall Community figures for Spain and Portugal.

Source: Economic activity rates, Labour Force Survey, 1985

However, the lifelong class engendered differences in the enjoyment of health and income are exaggerated in retirement.

In saying this, we should acknowledge that we know little about the proportion of people who are unhappy in their later working lives. Cribier (1980), however, found that a majority of Parisian salaried workers, interviewed in 1975, thought that retirement was desirable provided that income was adequate and health good. Among the 25 per cent of her respondents who had been retired for more than two years and who were not satisfied, income remained the primary reason for dissatisfaction. Money plays a key role in providing access to other resources in retirement: a point illustrated by Cribier's finding that people on the lowest incomes were the most socially isolated.

Health is the second factor which consistently shows a significant and positive association with attitudes to retirement. Beck's longitudinal study of men in the United States found health to be of overwhelming importance in retirement satisfaction (Beck, 1983). For some groups of people, poor health may also be associated with early retirement and with their dissatisfaction with retirement. Those who retire early on health grounds, have often been in low paid manual employment, and thus face a retirement which they have not sought or prepared for, suffering from low incomes and chronic ill health or disability (Laczko et al, 1988). Not surprisingly, their experience of retirement tends to be negative.

A third group who frequently show negative attitudes to retirement are those made compulsorily redundant ahead of their expected time of retirement.

If these are the major problems which may be faced by people in retirement, how are they to be helped to confront and deal with them? Much PFR is still geared to the two day course, a model which stubbornly persists, especially when it is provided by an outside agency. But neither health nor income are matters which can be significantly affected by a short course, held a few weeks before retirement. Good health in later life is something which needs to be prepared for years in advance. Indeed, one of the most telling comments in our enquiries came from a retired person in Spain who said 'If I'd known I was going to live this long I'd have looked after my health earlier'.

This is not to say that health promotion is not valuable at any age. We recognise that the participants in a PFR course are a good captive audience. Health advice at this stage, however, should be secondary to more fundamental strategies to promote good health from a much earlier age in workplaces, homes and the wider environment. Factors such as health and safety at work may be more important than individual preventive health activities. The latter may be of more significance in the area of mid-life planning than for people on the brink of retirement. In addition it should not be forgotten that, while good health in retirement is of crucial importance, there is the danger, in emphasising the possibilities of illness, that the image of old age as a period of decrepitude may be reinforced.

Many of these points about health apply to financial planning for retirement, since this is an area where some people can take effective action. The opportunity to plan in this way, however, may be limited by people's earnings and financial resources. Major pension planning obviously has to precede retirement by at least ten years. There are, however, two areas in which financial advice can be effective in PFR.

First, there is the matter of advice on the additional social security benefits to which people may be entitled. Obviously, given rapid changes in the regulations governing such benefits, advice needs to be immediate rather than long term, and there will always be some people who will benefit from this kind of information on retirement. It should be recognised, however, that welfare rights education should not be limited to the time of retirement. Many people need advice much earlier than retirement age regarding their pension entitlements, if they are to avoid discovering too late that their contribution records are insufficient (Glendenning and Pearson, 1988). Welfare benefits education is also likely to be needed following retirement. Many people may have looked into their entitlements on retirement, concluded that they were not eligible for anything, and have assumed that this will continue to be the case thereafter, oblivious to changes both in regulations and in their own circumstances. They will need to be constantly alert to the significance of such changes for their rights to benefits throughout their retirement.

An increasing number of people are retiring, or being made redundant, with a fairly substantial lump sum of money. A second area of advice is in regard to investment, particularly to people with no previous experience of handling large sums of money. This may be of considerable importance and it is because of this, as will be discussed later, that financial institutions and financial advisors have become involved in PFR.

A positive role for PFR

What can people be offered to help them prepare for their retirement? Retired people are free to develop new role models for retirement. PFR can give them the opportunity to explore possible roles in advance of their actual retirement. In France, however, it has been argued that help should be given shortly *after* people finish work, when they have had the time to experience the realities of retirement.

Because there are still few role models available for this new phase of life, it is important that people should be given some help to understand the options available. Thereafter, however, they should be encouraged and helped to make their own choices, rather than being given a series of cut and dried prescriptions (see Hagestad, 1981). Retirement is a significant period of transition in people's lives and good PFR will enable them to use their existing skills in dealing with change, or to develop new skills to handle the alterations which retirement brings to their lives.

Although what we have proposed so far reflects an ideal model, it follows from our perception of the nature of retirement at the present time. How then does it match with current provision for PFR?

Current PFR provision

In reviewing current PFR provision, it must be remembered that we were not able to carry out any systematic study of the *amount* of PFR carried out in different countries. Rather, we concentrated on identifying different aspects of practice.

PFR has been provided in the United Kingdom for over thirty years, starting with some early work in the West Midlands and in Scotland. This early work drew upon advice (which is still pertinent today) from a working party of the National Old People's Welfare Council (Heron, 1961). This led to the formation of the Pre-Retirement Association (PRA). A further impetus, which originated in other European countries, was the 'discovery' in the 1970s of the 'Third Age', the period between finishing full time work and the onset of dependency in old age (Weers, 1980; de Wijs, 1981-2; Fulgraff, 1986). Perhaps more significantly, interest in PFR grew when certain industries and large employers began shedding older workers, through various forms of early retirement. This development followed the oil crisis of the early seventies and the development of microtechnology.

In 1977, a Council of Europe Working Party, in reviewing PFR, described it as a developing scene. Our enquiries, however, which are similarly reliant on such published information as is available, suggest that there has been little expansion, and that, in some countries, PFR activity has even contracted (Council of Europe, 1977; Pearson et al., forthcoming).

Most PFR is provided through courses but there are other strategies, for example, phased retirement schemes. However, these have declined recently among individual firms although some governments, like Denmark, have set up schemes to promote partial retirement (Swank,

1982, 1983; Moller, 1987).

PFR courses vary between (i) concentrated sessions of one or two days, (ii) one session a week over several weeks, and (iii) weekend or week long residential sessions. There are four main types of agency that provide courses.

National pre-retirement organisations. In France, Ireland and the United Kingdom, there are specific national pre-retirement organisations offering courses to employers and the general public, as well as generally seeking to stimulate PFR. Additonally, there are 44 local PRA groups in the United Kingdom, generally independent affiliates of the national body. A similar network exists in Ireland but not, except for a few local PFR groups, in France. In Belgium, Denmark and Spain there are national and regional organisations concerned with elderly people which offer PFR courses as part of their overall programmes.

Adult education agencies. PFR work is also done by adult education agencies. In Germany, Denmark and the Netherlands, folk high schools provide courses. A third of adult education institutions in England offer courses. The motivation for provision appears to have varied between a genuine interest in the subject and a need to replenish the colleges' programmes after the collapse of the traditional apprenticeship courses. In France, there is some tradition for paid educational leave (PEL) following legislation in 1971. However, despite a government levy on firms to pay for the scheme, by no means all firms actually make use of it. Of those who do, most use the scheme for vocational and technical training, though it can be used for PFR and a small part of the scheme is deployed in this way. In Spain and France there is some provision by social services agencies.

Pension firms. As we have already noted, personal pension schemes are becoming more prevalent in the United Kingdom and Spain, and to a lesser extent in France. They may also expand in Denmark in the near future. This development generally reflects an anxiety on the part of governments to offload public expenditure commitments. Simultaneously, the promotion of personal pensions schemes generates widespread concern that state pension schemes will not deliver an adequate level of

101

pension in the future. In consequence, some pension firms, such as the Prudential and Allied Dunbar in the United Kingdom and PFA pensions in Denmark, have also entered the field of PFR offering half, one or two day 'off the peg' packages. Not surprisingly, these concentrate on financial matters, and this raises important questions about how disinterested the advice that is offered may be. Smaller independent financial advisers are also offering courses, or components of larger courses. In France, some of the *caisses de retraite* (pension schemes which complement basic state provision) have been offering PFR courses as part of their service to future beneficiaries. Sometimes they meet the full costs themselves, from their Social Action Divisions, seeing PFR as a means of reducing demand for their social work and domiciliary services for pensioners. In other cases, the *caisses*, may share costs with the employer's compulsory training fund. However, because there are different *caisses* for basic workers and managers, with separate contribution schemes related to salaries, PFR courses are more likely to be provided for managerial staff. Once again this maintains existing inequalities at work into retirement.

Employers. Finally, but very significantly, there are courses and other forms of preparation provided directly by employers themselves. Coleman (1982) found that less than 6 per cent of all employers in England and Wales offered PFR courses, of whom 60 per cent arranged the programme themselves. During the 1980s, many more private agencies have entered the field. There is some evidence to suggest that the amount of PFR provided by employers has diminished in recent years. There was a boom at the time when many firms were making mass redundancies and felt that they could soften the blow by offering at least the semblance of concern for their departing employees; this was especially so in France. Now that most of those redundancies have been made, and that a 'new realism' is the order of the day in industry, there appears to be a reduction in staff welfare provision generally, and this includes PFR. We found a number of firms in France and the United Kingdom where the welfare or personnel sections, which had organised PFR, were now fighting to maintain it against managerial calls for evidence of 'value for money'.

Most PFR initiatives are led by employers. It follows that whether or not they are directly providing the courses, it is the employers, rather than those who are retiring, who need to be convinced of the benefits of PFR.

This may have implications for the philosophy, content and style of courses, and the scope for innovation in course planning. While the format of courses may vary substantially, there is likely to be a premium on short, sharp, information based courses, rather than on long term, reflective, student led discussions. Short, didactic courses are easy to arrange, especially if bought in as a package, and they do not raise too many awkward questions about 'life', inside or outside work. They tend to promote a model of retirement as a new, discrete phenomenon which occurs after one's working life is over, rather than as an opportunity to draw upon experience and raise questions about the quality of life at work.

One factor, which may modify the unwillingness of employers to support PFR, is the attitude of trade unions. PFR may be accepted, and indeed has been accepted, by some unions as part of the social wage. Unions in Denmark, Spain and the United Kingdom have all stated that they consider PFR a responsibility of the employer, though it may not necessarily take high priority in their demands on employers. In Spain, although less than 10 per cent of the workforce is unionised, the unions, expressing their concern with living conditions in retirement, did organise a general strike in 1987 in protest against proposed changes in pensions. Some British trade unions have similarly treated the decline in the value of the state earnings related pension (SERPS) as an urgent issue. The Trades Union Congress in the United Kingdom has produced a model agreement on PFR for use in local negotiations, but we do not know to what extent it has actually been adopted.

Who receives PFR?

Next, we ask who is being reached by PFR. On the whole, they are employees in large firms, those with over 500 employees. The reasons are fairly obvious. Such firms are more likely to be able to give their employees time off, and will also have enough staff retiring at any one time to justify the setting up of a specific course. Smaller employers often have to rely on the availability of a course, for example, at an adult education agency. This could be a factor in explaining national variations in the provision of PFR. In Denmark, for example, most people work in small firms, while some of the larger firms, which have recently developed in fields such as electronics, have a predominantly young workforce with few people as yet reaching retirement age.

There is little firm data on occupational class, but it seems that white collar staff and managers are more likely to be offered courses by their employers and by pension funds. As in adult education generally, those attending PFR courses for the general public are more likely to be middle class. The one exception to this tendency are courses specifically for those made redundant. They are more likely to be attended by manual workers, but this group may decrease if redundancy programmes themselves decline. This may help to explain the decline in some areas of PFR work in France and, perhaps, in other countries.

Take up varies considerably between men and women. At Folk High Schools in Denmark and Germany, there is a higher proportion of women than men on PFR, as on other courses (Fulgraff, 1986). By contrast, Coleman (1982) found that men were more likely than women to attend PFR courses in the United Kingdom. This was true even allowing for the fact that, on a third of the courses he studied, participants were invited to bring along their (generally female) partners. Low participation by women may also be explained by difficulties in attending due to family commitments, especially if courses are residential. Added to this, eligibility criteria often discriminate against part time workers, and against those who have worked for their firms for less than a certain number of years. Thus it should not be surprising that women in the United Kingdom participate less frequently than do men (Shortland, 1985). In France, on the other hand, where all employees are required to contribute to supplementary *caisses de retraite*, women are as likely as men to be able to attend a course. This is dependent, however, upon their *caisse* having enough funds in its Social Action Division and, as we have seen already, this tends to maintain inequalities between managers and basic workers.

A few agencies, such as PiZ in the Netherlands, have been taking seriously the anxieties which women may feel about the threat to their own autonomy which is posed by their husbands' retirement. Some PiZ courses, like some courses in France, have asked each partner on a course to compare their expectations of retirement. Their perceptions are invariably different, and they can then be helped to explore them and to work out new strategies together (Scheffer, 1981-2). As a new development, some courses are being run in France, the Netherlands and the United Kingdom for women who are not in paid employment. These explore role changes which women experience in later middle age, as well as preparing them for their partners' retirements. Developments of this nature, of course, have to be based in the community, rather than organised by employers.

One group of people whose interests have largely been ignored at retirement are migrant workers, of whom an increasing number are working in the European Community. One notable exception is Renault in France. At first, the Renault management were unwilling to consider a separate course for their predominantly North African migrant workers. They became convinced, however, that there were real differences in practical, legal and pensions details, as well as in relationships and family life. These courses appear to have gone well. This issue of migrant workers is likely to become more significant after 1992.

Current issues in PFR

Finally, we turn to some current key issues. First is the question of timing for PFR programmes. Some firms, such as Shell UK, offer a two day financial session ten years before retirement. The firm, RTZ, also in the United Kingdom, has introduced a seminar five years before retirement and a three day course within the last two years. Another United Kingdom firm that has gone for early provision is Ford who, at Dagenham, are now offering mid-life planning courses to their middle managers.

Several PFR organisations which provide courses would favour the idea of earlier provision but, as we have noted already, these decisions are in the hands of employers, and generally they still send people for PFR in their last working year. We should also note that the association of PFR with redundancy has tended to engender workers' suspicions about their employers' motives. This has had a generally deleterious effect upon uptake of courses which are planned well ahead of expected retirement age.

Moreover, some organisations in France and Denmark have been finding that people often enrol for courses six months after retirement, when they realise that there are more issues in retirement than just financial ones. Bearing in mind the problems discussed earlier, of courses being initiated by employers, this observation raises questions about *where* courses should be based. There are obvious advantages to having them in workplaces where people due to retire can be easily contacted, but there is also a strong case for courses being based in the community. This is that PFR should link into the local community, emphasising the continuities of retirement in the lives of those who, after all, may have been living in the same community for many years. This approach may also serve as a starting point for integrating retired people into retirement (Lansley and Pearson, forthcoming).

Possibly, the most pertinent issue is that of the educational methods employed on PFR courses. Some people would question the ability of shop-floor workers to participate effectively in open discussion sessions. Others, however, can cite examples of such work and, with equal vehemence, question the didactic methods which present retirement as a cut and dried phenomenon and which deny the problem solving skills which people build up over their lifetimes.

This debate goes to the heart of the issues which we raised earlier about the function of PFR. Is it to provide people with standard information about certain problematic areas of retirement, or is it to help them to build their own transitional bridges to the next major period of their lives? The effectiveness of the first approach, as we have seen, is limited, not only by the time constraints under which it operates, but more importantly because of the wider structural conditions under which many retired people lead their lives. The second appears perhaps to be utopian and, it could be argued, it belongs more properly to the field of educational gerontology than to PFR. It does, however, address itself more relevantly to the real interests of retired and retiring people. How it is to be achieved remains an open question, but we can offer one or two suggestions from our research.

Pre-retirement organisations. PFR activity appears to be most prevalent where there are structures, like the PRA in the United Kingdom, specifically committed to it. Local networks, as well as national agencies, may be significant in this. Where PFR has just been provided for a specific purpose, such as dealing with issues of redundancy, once the immediate need has passed provision may fall back again.

Adult education. The model which we would advocate, of PFR helping the participant to explore possibilities of personal development in

106

retirement, requires links between PFR and other areas of adult education. This carries the need for governmental support for adult education, and particularly that which is targetted upon the general public and third age people.

Paid educational leave. Given the limits on employer support, and the additional problems of small firms, there may be a need for statutory support for paid educational leave, and for PFR to be a component in this. This will not come voluntarily from employers, and thus requires the commitment of governments and, until such commitment is available, of trade unions. All parties need to recognise that paid educational leave (PEL) has a contribution to offer to personal development, as well as to technical training.

Transferable entitlements. Some American firms will pay the course fees of members of their staff employed in branches too far away to participate in their own PFR programmes, not only for local adult education PFR courses but also for other leisure interest courses. The aim is to help staff to develop non-work interests. This could be linked in to our proposal for PEL, and might give people transferable entitlements within the European Community which were not dependent on time spent with one particular firm or on variations in policy between plants in different countries.

Women and migrants. The issues concerning women and migrant workers are both important. Some creative work is now developing for women; almost invariably it is set in a community context rather than a work setting. There is a dilemma here. Without employer support widespread take up is unlikely, but PFR may be more effective in a community rather than a workplace context. The needs of migrant workers require a lot more study, particularly as the European Community opens up further to trans-national employment.

Health and income. Finally, PFR is not a substitute for low pension levels, or for poor health in retirement. These remain the two crucial issues for satisfaction in retirement, and must be addressed separately by governments. PFR is not a strategy for encouraging people either to

107

adjust to the indefensible way in which retirement compounds existing work inequalities, or to ignore the real solutions to health and income inequalities in terms of improving working conditions and wages.

Acknowledgement

This paper is based on a study commissioned by the European Community and carried out during 1987-8 (Pearson et al, forthcoming). Inevitably we were not able to do an in-depth study in the short time available to us, and we had to rely heavily on published sources, with visits and interviews with key informants in four member states selected as case studies: Denmark, France, Spain and the United Kingdom.

9 Promoting health changes in later life: the Self Health Care Project

Miriam Bernard and Vera Ivers

This action research project is jointly sponsored by the Beth Johnson Foundation and the European Community under the second programme to combat poverty.

The Beth Johnson Foundation is a charitable trust set up in 1972 specifically to help improve the quality of life of older people. It achieves this aim through innovative developments with and for older people, and through research related to ageing. It has been working with older people in an effort to help them to find new and satisfying ways of using the time available to them in retirement. This work has included setting up what is now a thriving Leisure Association that is organising various sporting activities throughout the week, and initiating a Senior Centre. In the centre, people can take part in groups ranging from painting to 'popagility' and there are opportunities to meet and make new friends.

Within these projects, and as a result of discussion groups held at the Senior Centre, it became increasingly obvious that an additional element to the work should emphasise health education and promotion. Immediately before retirement, many seem to worry enormously about the level of their income and how they will manage but, within a few months of having retired, they switch to worry about their health and how they might stay independent and active for as long as possible.

The Self Health Care Project

The Self Health Care Project is firmly rooted in the Foundation's earlier experiences of developing and researching leisure opportunities, education and health related activities for older people. It aims to provide an accessible, attractive and popular means of furthering health education and health promotion amongst a group of people who are not generally the target of such initiatives. This is in a setting which is as far removed as possible from the formal clinical settings in which health care is usually offered.

The project's underlying principles are:

- to help raise older people's awareness of health care and health maintenance;

- to encourage the involvement of more older people in health care programmes;

- to assist older people in identifying their health needs and developing the skills and strategies required to obtain resources to meet these needs.

Senior Health Shop

The project has four components. First there is the Senior Health Shop. This is sited near to the city centre shopping precinct and close to the bus station, so that it is possible for people to call in on their way to or from a shopping trip. The shop is bright and attractive and inside there is a large display of colourful health literature. There are two paid members of staff, one a qualified nurse. The front of the shop is set out as a small cafeteria with attractive table covers and comfortable chairs. Older volunteers prepare and serve a variety of nutritious snacks and drinks, all of which have been approved by the district dietician. Volunteers meet clients when they come into the shop for a cup of coffee or to pick up some leaflets. They have become skilled in recognising when someone wants to talk about a problem and is finding it difficult to make the first move. Volunteers can then suggest, when they are serving the cup of coffee, that it may be helpful to talk to one of the staff. The staff will then offer personal counselling or advice, and may offer practical help in the form of introductions to appropriate groups. There is also a 'walk in' blood pressure checking service, a chance to be weighed regularly, and computerised health programmes.

Peer health counsellors

The second component involves counselling. Peer health counsellors are older volunteers who have themselves taken an interest in health maintenance. They are at the stage when they feel they would like to pass on some of their enthusiasm to others in their age group. The volunteers are trained quite intensively and this involves a residential period. The training examines long held beliefs about health, misconceptions and 'old wives tales'. Much of it, however, is concerned with communication and, alongside that, is intended to raise the confidence of volunteers in order that they might pass on their enthusiasm.

Once trained, peer health counsellors work in a number of ways. Some help individuals, either those who have come into the shop or senior centre or those they have met at a health fair or exhibition. They offer individual advice and support, sometimes over a considerable period of time while the person is attempting to reorganise his or her life. Others work in small groups, visiting residential homes for elderly people or sheltered housing schemes. Here, they lead discussion programmes and exercise programmes with residents or tenants, and this is becoming a much sought after service, especially within the residential care setting. Staff often feel that residents need something more stimulating than the usual routine of feeding, cleaning and sleeping. They do not have the time to offer it themselves or even, perhaps, do not feel they have permission to use their time in this way. Volunteers also bring a new dimension to relationships in the home, and staff often tell us of immediate and quite dramatic changes that occur as a result of these visits.

Plans are currently under way for peer health counsellors to attend, on a regular basis, doctors' surgeries and health clinics. There, they will invite patients over 50 years of age to learn something about health care maintenance programmes. Patients will come either through recommendations from the doctors, or through the publicity material displayed in the surgery.

Peer health counsellors also attend special events arranged for retired people, such as retirement exhibitions and health fairs, where they staff a special stand offering literature and advice.

Health activities

The third element of the project is the provision of health related courses and activities. These mainly consist of groups that are operating within the Senior Centre or under the wing of the Beth Johnson Leisure Association. However, three courses were instituted at the Senior Centre directly as a result of enquiries and problems presented at the Senior Health Shop. The first of these three courses is 'Look After Yourself' which is tutored by a lecturer seconded from a local college of further education. The lecturer also runs a nutrition class and a stress management class.

Other activities to which people can be referred are 'popagility', yoga, regular swimming classes, rambling, badminton, table tennis, bowling and general keep fit. The Senior Centre has a number of other, more sedentary, pursuits on offer as well. Apart from the activities organised under the umbrella of the Beth Johnson Foundation, the Senior Health Shop and peer health counsellors make available material and information on other courses, classes and activities in and around the city.

CAREline

The fourth element of the scheme is called 'CAREline'. This is a telephone link scheme aimed at frail housebound elderly people who are deemed to be at risk. The telephone is staffed every afternoon by two peer health counsellors who phone out to a list of clients who have been referred by social workers, nurses, health visitors, doctors or carers. Some of these people may have been recently discharged from hospital, others may be on waiting lists for a long-term bed. All of them are extremely frail and vulnerable. The volunteer's call each day serves as an excellent monitoring system: checking on whether they have eaten, slept, taken their drugs, and whether anything untoward has happened to them over the previous twenty-four hours. It is also a breath of life for these people, offering them the opportunity to chat to someone about other things and generally get the feel of the outside world. Occasionally, for example at Christmas, the volunteers and some of the clients who are well enough, meet face to face, and this always proves to be a successful event.

When referrals are made, one of the staff, or a volunteer who has been specially trained, visits the client to assess the degree of need. In this way we hope to keep the service operating for those who are truly at risk. It is not meant to be a service to those who are lonely. The visitor will also check practical details such as how far the telephone is from the armchair, the bed or the bathroom. In some cases we have had to ask for the telephone to be moved to improve accessibility. Telephone calls are made only on those days when no one else will be contacting the person. Consequently, some people may be called each day, others may be called two to three times a week.

A crucial element in this service is the back-up available from a professional worker. CAREline currently runs from a small office at the back of the Senior Health Shop, so there is always someone available who can accept responsibility, should a problem arise. Obviously, a recurrent problem is when a very frail and housebound person does not answer the telephone. To deal with this, we always insist on the name and telephone number of a key person. This person might be a relative, or a social worker, or someone at the local clinic. When the volunteers get no reply, they ring at half hourly intervals during the afternoon. At the end of the afternoon, if they have not been able to raise the client, they will call the key person. If that person cannot be raised, and there is still some doubt as to the well being of the client, we have a standing offer from the community police to go and investigate. We have not so far had to use this service, but it has always been reassuring to know that we could.

One CAREline office, with two volunteers and access to a back up worker, can monitor forty people each day. We are looking at the possibility of starting another CAREline group, rather than increasing the number of calls from the existing base. There are various reasons for this. It would be difficult to have more than two telephone lines operating from one office and the time at which calls are made is quite crucial. We start calls at 1 p.m., when the reduced rate applies with British Telecom, and we aim to finish them by 4 p.m., when volunteers often wish to go because of cheaper bus fares.

Monitoring the project

This project is the first opportunity the Foundation has had to monitor a development through its lifetime. With previous projects, our monitoring has tended to be mainly retrospective. This time, we are engaged in an action research project in which results are periodically fed back, so that we can manage and develop the project on a day by day basis. In order to do this, the monitoring is organised around a broad framework. There are three parts to this.

- *The process of development.* Prior to, and throughout the project's lifetime, detailed records are being kept to produce a chronology of its development. This will describe the details of how it is organised and run from day to day. Apart from providing an ongoing account, this is important for others who may want to learn from what we are doing, or to borrow elements of it.

- We are gathering a variety of *quantitative information*, to provide some 'hard' facts about the people who become involved in the project and its various components. This will aid our exploration of some of the outcomes of the project. For example, we hope to determine who the project has reached and what effect it is having on them.

- *Qualitative details.* Here, we are attempting to discover in more depth, what the project means to individuals in the context of their life experiences.

Quantitative information

In the remainder of this paper, we will focus on the second element: the quantitative information. Because we have four components to the project, we employ a variety of methods to gather quantitative information. At the shop, for example, we have short forms on all the

114

tables for customers to complete. We keep a daily diary, and, four times a year we hold what we call a census week. We also keep track of all our volunteers and of the work they do in peer health counselling or with CAREline clients. On training or health-related courses, we keep registers and ask participants to complete feedback forms and evaluation sheets. This obviously yields a wealth of information, but we shall confine this discussion to some of the findings relating to the shop, and to the census weeks in particular.

We began our census weeks in March 1987 and to date (September 1988) have carried out seven in total. During 1987, these weeks had two main aims, firstly to produce a total count or census of everyone who came through the door of the shop, and, secondly, to conduct face to face interviews with every second visitor. Our interviews made use of a simple four page questionnaire which asked for social and personal information about customers, how they heard about the shop, why they had come, what aspects of health they were interested in, and what they planned to do, or perhaps had already done, to improve their health. We also asked for their opinions about the shop and what other kinds of services, advice or health related groups might be of interest to them. In 1988, we have changed the questionnaire to a shorter self completion format. What then has all this information told us about the people we are reaching?

Table 9-1 presents total attendances at the shop. From this, it is evident that attendance has been steadily increasing. In the first twelve

Table 9-1 *Senior Health Shop attendances*

Nov.	1986	379	Nov.	1987	629
Dec.	"	269	Dec.	"	450
Jan.	1987	232	Jan.	1988	835
Feb.	"	347	Feb.	"	793
Mar.	"	387	Mar.	"	979
Apr.	"	402	Apr.	"	885
May	"	348	May	"	843
June	"	411	June	"	1110
July	"	489	July	"	884
Aug.	"	508	Aug.	"	1015
Sept.	"	717			
Oct.	"	577			
TOTALS		5066	(to date)		8423

months, we had just over 5,000 visitors, while in the last ten months this has already exceeded 8,000.

During the six census weeks which have been subject to analysis (the seventh was held earlier this month), we have interviewed a total of 399 people aged 50 or over: 19 per cent were men and 81 per cent women. Although their ages range from 50 to 87, nearly two thirds of our customers are aged between 50 and 65 years. So, although we are attracting a very wide age span, the emphasis is on the newly or early retired and on those not in paid employment.

The imbalance reflected in the sex ratio is also apparent in the other socio-demographic information we have about them. We know, for example, that two fifths of the sample are widowed. In addition, two fifths of the women live alone and almost half of them survive on an income of less than £50 per week: in essence on the basic state pension.

Our custom then, is dominated by unemployed and retired women aged between the ages of 50 and 65, many of whom are widowed and living on low incomes. These findings are important because they reveal that our project is reaching a section of the population who, research has shown, tend to under-consult the formal primary health services (Hannay, 1979). In fact, Ford and Taylor (1985) contend that, on the basis of available

Table 9-2 *Comparison of Senior Health Shop with more formal health services (percentages)*

	Male	Female	Total
More friendly, relaxed and informal	29	25	25
Easy to obtain information leaflets	14	17	16
Have time to sit and talk	9	14	13
Can call in at any time	2	10	12
Unthreatening	9	11	11
Easier to talk here	-	7	6
It's women, not men	-	6	5
Food available	9	3	4
Other	29	28	28
DK/Can't say	-	3	3
Total (= 100%)	76	315	391

116

evidence, it is middle-aged women (in the age groups 30-44 and 45-64) rather than those over 65 years who run the greatest risks in neglecting health problems.

So, how do people's experiences of the shop compare with their experiences of more formal health services? We ask this in the form of an open ended question which, as is apparent from Table 9-2, has attracted a wide variety of responses. Most frequently mentioned were the friendly, relaxed and informal nature of the shop, and the ease of obtaining information and leaflets. A number of the women also felt that it was easier to talk in the shop and they liked the fact that women were present, a pointer to their under-utilisation of formal services.

In order to put some flesh on the bones of these categories, the following are examples of their comments:

Friendliness

It's more free and easy and informal.

It's more personal here.

It's got a friendly atmosphere.

Information/leaflets

It's a helpful place for leaflets.

Information and leaflets are available and you're not pestered by anyone.

You're able just to take leaflets.

Time to sit/talk

You have more time to be able to talk. Doctors write prescriptions before they know what you've got, and you feel as if you're taking someone else's time up.

You can meet people who have the time to talk to you.

The staff are willing to sit and talk - not like the GPs where you're in and out with a written prescription.

117

Table 9-3 *Health concerns (percentages)*

	Male	Female	Total
Healthy, good diet	35	34	34
Exercise	43	20	25
Specific condition	14	20	19
eg arthritis; stroke; blood pressure			
Weight	7	18	16
Stress control	–	18	14
General interest	14	13	13
Keeping active	–	7	6
Other	–	7	6
TOTAL (= 100%)	46	189	234

Call in

There are no waiting lists here.

GPs are very busy, but you can call in any time here.

You can come in when you want.

Unthreatening

I'm not frightened to come in here and talk, but I am frightened to go to the doctor's.

I wouldn't be frightened to ask questions here.

I'm scared of doctors.

Easier to talk

It's more free and easy, and you're more likely to tell people how you feel, and be able to discuss things more fully.

It's easy to ask things here.

Women

More women can talk in a shop like this.

118

It's women here, and you can't talk to doctors because most of
them are men.

Why do people and particularly women come to the shop, and what are
they gaining from it? Table 9-3 shows that about a third of respondents
are interested in healthy food and in eating a healthier diet, about a
quarter are interested in exercise, and a fifth have a specific condition they
are concerned about such as arthritis or blood pressure. We also ask our
customers whether their visits to the shop have either prompted them into

---

Table 9-4 *Reactions to visits*

First time visitors	Previous visitors
Diet	
I have high cholesterol and want to change my diet.	I now eat less meat, more fish, and use wholemeal flour.
I want to eat more fibre.	I had wholemeal scones here and liked them, so I now buy
I need to think more about flour. my diet.	wholemeal flour, not white
	I eat less sugar and have decaffeinated coffee.
Exercise/Activity	
I want to do more exercise coming but I don't know exactly what yet. disease.	I took up yoga again after here and find the relaxation is good for my Parkinson's
I'd like to take up swimming.	I've started dancing.
I want to go walking or rambling.	I'm joining a relaxation class later this month, and the rambling group.
Stress	
I want to learn how to overcome stress problems.	I've joined the ramblers club and the walks have helped me in handling stress.

thinking more about their health or into actually taking any action and, if it has, to tell us what this relates to. About half of our respondents replied positively to these questions.

As a general rule, first time visitors talk in terms of what they intend to do, or what they would like to do. Those who have visited us over a period of time, perhaps talked with staff and volunteers, and picked up and read a variety of literature, are able to tell us what concrete changes they have made. Table 9-4 presents some illustrative comments.

Conclusion

In essence, what the project is doing is attempting to facilitate the process whereby older people can increasingly take charge of themselves and their lives. We are not, by any stretch of the imagination, seeking to create a substitute for formal health services. However, what our results are beginning to show is that we are tending to cater for a group who, for a variety of reasons, are neglected by the formal health service. The following concluding comments illustrate best how our project, and the shop in particular, complements existing services.

You can pick up natural things here - there are no drugs being pushed.

It feels like a half-way house before going to the GP - for self-help rather than drugs.

It's a good start because you can walk in, look round and walk out again, but it does start you thinking.

10 'Only old women': emerging issues in feminist groupwork

Pat Le Riche and Chloe Rowlings

The work described in this paper has its roots in the authors' long term commitment to working with older women, and the recognition of the need for further 'research and theory development to clarify the relationship between macro level social arrangements and individual subjective experience' (Evers, 1985).

Central to our argument is the conviction that the development of a feminist analysis of social work must emphasise the need to destigmatize and empower women as users of social work services and to encourage a collaborative style of work. Feminist writers such as Wise (1985) have emphasised the need for involvement and change on the part of the worker as well as the client, while recent studies (e.g. Donnelly, 1986) have demonstrated how groupwork can lead women to feel strong enough to change their lives within both the domestic and political spheres. Aspects of our own analysis go some way towards establishing an initial framework of relations between the personal and the political. However, while groupwork has long been established as a means of offering mutual support to younger women, we feel that such an approach is often overlooked in work with women in older age groups. As Finch and

Groves (1985) have argued, practice continues to be dominated by age and gender stereotypes. Indeed, organisational ageism and sexism, the influence of the organisation and the groupwork process, and the issues of power and control, are all central to an understanding of the groupwork described in this paper.

Our involvement with the two groups we describe raised many difficult questions about the use and value of groupwork with older women. For example, while there was a clear advantage in setting up a discussion group to meet the affective needs of its members, the absence of a perceived need for discussion - which may be associated with depressing or forbidden topics - often proved threatening to potential members. One of the group explained that personal information and opinions were often shared after art classes or scrabble games, yet it was precisely this stereotypical approach to groupwork with older people which we were attempting to avoid. However, in the final analysis it was our own preconceptions which were being challenged, and it seems clear that workers must be prepared to accept, share and understand the strong and often negative emotions which they are likely to encounter.

The leaders are either presumed to be omniscient, because they too are women, or to be ineffectual because they are 'only women' in a society which tends to place men in key roles (Eichenbaum and Orbach, 1982). This seems particularly important for all women working with women.

The limitations of social work practice with older women

There is a small but increasingly significant literature describing social work practice with older women. The scene was set by writers such as Rowlings (1981) and Marshall (1983) who highlighted the poor quality of service received by older people who became clients of social services departments. Stereotyped assumptions about older people's needs reflected the separation and marginalisation of pensioners in society. As a result, Stevenson and Parsloe (1978) and Rowlings (1981) describe how social workers perceive work with older people as unrewarding and limited to service provision. Against this background, imaginative and creative responses to older people as social work clients have been slow to emerge. Similarly, Phillipson (1981) has shown how the women's

122

movement focused its attention mostly on the impact of inequality and disadvantage on younger women.

It is only gradually, as women within the movement begin to age, that the 'double jeopardy' of ageism and sexism as experienced by older women has come to be appreciated (Itzin 1984). In the fields of income maintenance, housing and caring, for example, Peace (1986) has shown that social policy has enhanced rather than removed the inequalities experienced by women throughout their lifetime, and that these are exacerbated as women age. Government policies have emphasised the 'problem' of ageing without devising welfare programmes which would prevent or remedy the disadvantages experienced by pensioners, particularly by the very old who are overwhelmingly women.

The recent development and articulation of these ideas has begun to have some impact on social work with older women. Hudson (1985) has described some of the reasons why feminism, which would seem to be in sympathy with social work goals and values, has failed to make more impact on state social work. Writers on women's issues, however, have described work with older women which could be characterised as feminist, and there are some examples of practice with older women which, though not specifically feminist in approach, attempt to extend and improve social work practice with older people. The struggle to retain a feminist perspective against the background of pressure from organisational factors was to become an essential theme in our groupwork experience.

Feminist approaches to groupwork

The monograph by Donnelly (1986) already mentioned, describes the experience of social workers working alongside a group of younger women in North Braunston in Leicestershire. In this paper, Donnelly identifies some of the advantages of using groupwork as both a personal and political vehicle for change, and outlines some of the characteristics of groupwork from a feminist perspective. These characteristics include using the personal experience of women in the group as an illustration of structural disadvantage in terms of social relations and political power. She also describes the process of becoming involved with the women and listening to their views rather than imposing solutions from the safe distance of the professional role. Donnelly's account highlights the importance of having an organisational context which, if not sympathetic to some of the characteristics outlined, is at least open enough not to sabotage the process. This can be problematic in state welfare organisations where groupwork of all kinds (let alone groupwork for women by women) is frequently marginalised to being a private part-time activity by individuals who are committed or isolated within specialist posts. However, given the low status of older women within society and the subsequent low status of social work practice with older clients, the characteristics of feminist groupwork outlined above could be one way of providing the 'degree of optimism' about the capacity for changing our organisations which, Hudson (1985) argues, 'is perhaps one of the most fundamental prerequisites for feminist influenced social work practice'.

The prevailing methods of groupwork with older people used by social workers in field, residential and day care settings have quite different goals and approaches from the ones outlined here. There are several accounts of reminiscence as a focus of groupwork with pensioners. For example, Wright (1984) and Bornat (1985) have described the setting up and running of such groups, and the uses made of reminiscence by older people have been well summarised by Coleman (1986). Traditionally, day care provision has offered a wide range of groups for social support, educational purposes (such as health groups), and help in crises such as bereavement. However, the literature on discussion groups describes few attempts to offer a degree of control to older women. Froggatt (1985) writes of the need to listen to the voices of older women as a means of using their creativity to correct normative assumptions and negative stereotypes of ageing. Valk (1985) describes her use of groupwork within a geriatric hospital. She too uses creative writing, in this case poetry, as a means of enabling patients to begin to discuss a number of themes relevant to their past and present experience. However, Valk's work has been criticised by Rodwell (1985) for failing to take account of the need to place the group within its organisational context. In this respect the description offered by Cooper (1980) of groupwork in a hospital setting, though not written from a specifically feminist perspective, offers a useful account of the possibilities and constraints of setting up a discussion group for older people.

Different writers have therefore highlighted different aspects of groupwork with older women. In this paper we aim to draw together some of these elements which emerged during our work with two groups in different settings.

The social services

In attempting to translate some of the work with women's groups to work with older women, we aimed to set up a discussion group which looked at issues such as women's experience of ageing and how other people treated them as individuals. In common with writers such as Donnelly (1986) and Froggatt (1985), we hoped the process would help women to become more self confident and feel supported by the shared experience of their peers. We planned to meet for five to ten sessions of one and a quarter hours in a social services office, with a group membership as varied as possible in terms of age and background - up to a maximum of ten members with two leaders. We took referrals from the social services' home care section, occupational therapists, local drop-in centres, social workers in the area office and local hospitals. We asked them to look for women who were over 65 years of age who were the clients of the Social Services Department or who had been clients within the previous two months. By targeting the group in this way, we hoped to achieve a broadly based membership with a range of past and present experiences, which would highlight strengths in coping as well as the more usual social work focus on problems and losses.

From the initial fourteen referrals we visited eight women. We also made contact with the local drop-in centre in the hope that some of its members would be interested in coming to the group. In the end we only recruited three women who became regular attenders. Partly because of this low take up and partly influenced by the structuring of reminiscence groups in the area, we decided to reduce the number of meetings to six. In terms of content, the groups had a pattern, beginning with looking back at what had happened during the past week. Initially, we saw this part of the meeting as an introduction, but frequently it took up most of the time.

Events taking place between meetings were very significant and this we had underestimated at the planning stage. For example, one member was forced to move house and another had to make visits to the hospital after

125

a major illness. It was inevitable that discussion of these issues took up a considerable amount of group time. We wanted the group's agenda to be flexible enough to enable the women to share experiences, gain support and meet their own needs. At times the women were responsive to this approach, but at others they appeared bewildered by this style of leadership and confused by the purpose of the group. Our discussions reflected the struggle the women were having to retain independence and control over their own way of life. We talked about health and the way women are treated by professionals and the different strategies they adopt for dealing with retirement, illness and disability. We looked at finance and housing and how to cope alone when friends and families are remote, either geographically or emotionally. At the end of the six sessions, the women felt the main advantage of our meetings had been the social and affective support they had received. All three women described themselves as lonely and we had learned from them of the significance of offering the opportunity to talk about what had happened in the past and what they were experiencing at the present. There appeared to be no other forum which enabled them to do this. 'It's all been very interesting and I won't have anywhere to go next Wednesday morning'. 'I've never been in a group before. What people like most is chatting, discussion - they like that better than anything'. 'People who are alone are so much deprived of speaking, of companionship and communication'.

The issues to emerge from this first group can be summarised under two main headings: leadership and organisational factors. In describing her work in setting up a women's study option on a social work course, McLeod (1987) describes some dilemmas similar to those we experienced. We have already described how the women expected us to control and organise the group. We, on the other hand, wanted to enable them to control the management of the group and determine the agenda. There was considerable tension in these differing expectations and at times the group members felt that we must have hidden goals and aims in mind, other than those we were sharing with them. It is not surprising in view of the status of older women that is reflected in social policy (Peace, 1986), that our group members found it hard to believe that anything that they had to say was important enough to be worth hearing. Since they knew we were social workers, they also expected us to be authoritative and resolve their problems, although we had discussed with them how we hoped to approach these issues at the beginning of the group.

There were less tangible differences in expectations which we gradually identified as the group progressed. Both the leaders have experience of being members of women's groups and therefore understood what was implied by the idea of 'a women's group', particularly the value of women meeting together which seemed self evident and which was an end in itself. This view was not shared by the older women in our group, nor did they feel we could share an understanding of their experience because we were women. This reflects the view expressed by Sutherland (1986), that it is naive to expect women to share 'common aspirations and experiences' regardless of differences in race, age and class. She quotes Rich 'the mere sharing of oppression does not constitute a common world'.

We had the advantage of hearing about the positive ways in which the group members coped with their difficulties, heard them support each other and discuss the ways in which their personal experiences related to the position of older women throughout society. Stanley and Wise (1979) and Oakley (1981) have described how it is impossible for women researchers to achieve and retain objectivity in their work with women. Were it possible, they argue, it would not be desirable. Similarly, in relation to our groupwork, the issue of negotiating appropriate boundaries was complex as we have already described. Our desire to adopt collaborative leadership styles and lower traditional professional boundaries, meant that we were frequently exposed to the painful experiences of older women in ways that made us sad and angry. The effect of this was to emphasise our own need for support from each other, from our supervision and from the women themselves.

Organisational issues

Our decision not to provide transport for the group was one of the main reasons for the small number of referrals we received. However, we also became aware of other factors which were equally significant. The area office was under pressure from statutory child care work and had a bias towards individual case work. We also found that work with older people was unpopular and seen to be unrewarding; it was not a high priority for qualified social work time (Rowlings, 1981; Marshall, 1983; Stevenson and

127

Parsloe, 1978). Our group, which was closer to a model of community development, was therefore outside the mainstream of social work in the area. Moreover it would have no noticeable effect on social workers' caseloads or duty work. Some workers were unable to see the need for a women's group and others lost interest when they found that only three women were attending. However, it seems probable that this lack of interest would have occurred even if the group had been larger. The issues themselves were not seen as important and there was an undercurrent of wanting the group to fail because success might have threatened existing styles of working. These problems seem to us to have been compounded by the prejudice against older people and against women which social work currently reflects.

Evaluation

When we came to evaluate the experience of the group with the members, they identified the support and opportunity for sharing as the most important aspect of the group for them. 'I'll miss the fact that I have a particular place to go. There is something I have to do and especially somewhere where I am able to voice my opinions'. 'I'll miss it'. These comments encouraged us to think that we could set up another group building on knowledge gained from this one. However, we identified important factors which needed to be addressed in the proces of setting up another group. In summary these were:

- the difficulty of getting referrals from an area office, particularly when transport was not offered;

- the differences in perspective between members and leaders which made aims and objectives difficult to clarify;

- the impact of ageism and sexism within organisations needs to be considered: organisational ageism and sexism will always be an essential concern when setting up groups for older women.

As leaders, we brought additional expectations based on our experience both with women and with social work professionals. We wanted an opportunity to listen to the women and learn from their experiences in a way which would enable us to improve the quality of our work as practitioners and trainers. 'Feminism reiterates that we must learn to listen to women instead of telling them what they want, what they are "really" like, and how they should be' (Donnelly, 1986).

Ash House

As the organisational factors had appeared to limit the referrals, the second group was run the following year in a local sheltered housing scheme called Ash House. We speculated that we might encounter a different range of needs than those identified by the women living alone. We thought that although it might be easier to recruit women to the group, the process would be complicated by the dynamics existing within Ash House. Our plan was for a closed group with similar aims, as the first group had encouraged us to agree with Donnelly (1986) that: 'the small group process both enhances the possibility of women learning about the link between personal experiences and the social structure and the resultant dichotomies and may also provide the support vital to encourage and sustain change in either one's self or one's situation'.

Ash House is run by a housing association which gives accommodation predominantly to older women. It is managed by two wardens who offer daily support, emergency cover for tenants and social activities. Social workers in the office where one of the leaders worked had a good and lengthy professional relationship with the wardens.

In describing the idea initially to the wardens, and then to the tenants, we used the term 'discussion group' and explained our roles as trainers or group workers rather than as social workers. However, we remained identified with the Social Services Department and, to the women, this seemed to imply that the group should only be for people with problems. At an early stage in the negotiations to set up the group, one woman said that she did not see herself as a priority for our time and attention, and that we should go and see the 'more needy people' who deserved greater help: 'We're not really a fair representation because we are alert and young in mind'.

Similarly the warden initially presented us with a potential group that was composed of tenants whose behaviour caused the most problems both for them and for the fitter tenants. These assumptions about our aims are

129

hardly surprising in view of the fact that their experience of social work within Ash House would have been associated with specific problems and the allocation of resources. We had also seen in the first group that the women frequently found it difficult to justify to themselves that they had a right to time and attention (Eichenbaum and Orbach 1982).

Possibly, they also imagined that we had a hidden 'therapeutic' agenda: 'You want something from us, we don't know yet. We're still in the dark'.

These doubts were discussed openly during our negotiations to set up the group and eventually appeared to have been resolved. However, they emerged later in the group process and remained significant issues.

As a result of our experiences with the first group, we had decided that we would not run a group with a membership of less than eight. In the event, twelve women expressed an interest in coming and we planned to hold ten, weekly sessions of one and a half hours in the afternoon. We returned to the idea of ten sessions, as six had not seemed long enough to do justice to the group's content and process.

Originally the Housing Association was intended to provide accommodation for single professional women and, to a large extent, this was reflected in the group's membership. The women felt that their current ability to retain their independence reflected a life's experiences. 'I think most elderly people are very independent, especially those who haven't been married'. Johnson's (1978) concept of 'seeing an individual life as a series of inter-related careers' seems relevant here, particularly in terms of each individual's ability to define her own needs.

The twelve women interested in the group were already part of an active social grouping at Ash House. Some were particularly active in the tenants association and in organising day to day activities. In terms of the categories of Evers (1985), these women could be described as 'active initiators' rather than 'passive responders'. They were a group who saw themselves as being in charge of their lives rather than as feeling that events that occurred were beyond their control. In the context of the overall dynamics at Ash House we were forming a new group from a number of existing groups. In the process of setting up the group we knew we had to pay particular attention to two main issues. First, with so many opportunities for social activity available, the women at Ash House might not feel the need for an additional chance to meet. In this respect, we tried to check out the members' commitment to attending another activity.

Secondly, the first group showed that a great openness was possible amongst those who could maintain some anonymity but who came together by choice. We recognised that it might be more difficult for women to share personal concerns and vulnerabilities with those with whom they lived. It was particularly important to assure them that material shared in the group would not be passed on to the wardens, as they were perceived as having the power to act on it.

Process and content

In spite of these difficulties, we felt, during the process of setting up the group, that they could be overcome. We hoped to achieve a regular membership of about eight women. We imagined that after the first few sessions the group would become more cohesive and secure. As it turned out, we negotiated the ending of the group after five sessions and during that time failed to achieve a satisfactory stability in either size or membership.

The first two meetings appeared to be successful and were well attended. The women were able to share the positive aspects of life at Ash House. 'We are all friendly and if necessary we help each other'. 'We have some very courageous people in this place ... they never give in'. Without much prompting, they were also able to share some of the real difficulties experienced by women of their age. 'I am old, but I am not decrepit'. 'The worse thing when you are old is to be patronised, and to feel that you are patronised'.

What they were not able to acknowledge were the more negative aspects of life at Ash House which related directly to themselves. We were later able to understand why they wished to detach themselves from these issues. A group established purely as a discussion group is likely to be difficult when the subjects of conversation are, directly or indirectly, death, decline and the loss of status, health and power. Matthews (1979) explains that 'old is not a pivotal self identity for most old people' who 'prefer to think that they are not old'. She argues that most old people use strategies for thinking of themselves as different, not 'typical' of their age group. They are put in that position by others.

However, after these two meetings the process of the group appeared to go wrong. The planning of the third meeting had been changed after much negotiation to accommodate a jumble sale which was due to coincide with our group's time. In spite of the leaders' feeling that the new timing was clear, no one turned up for this meeting. The leaders wrote an indignant letter to group members wondering why no one turned up. Two members came to the fourth meeting: one who was physically frail but lively, and another new member arriving for the first time. In this foursome we had an interesting discussion about issues such as the conditions of Ash House, but it in no way constituted a group meeting. Five members turned up for the fifth meeting. Discussion was mostly about the possible future of the group and, for the first time, the group members seemed to be honest about their lack of commitment to attend. 'I don't feel we get anywhere'. 'We really don't know what to say because what do they want from us'. 'I think you (the leaders) have got to talk more because you've got to get something out of us and we don't know what it is'. It was decided to end the group after this session and a letter was sent to all members past and present telling them of this decision.

Issues of power and control

> A feminist perspective points to the central issue in ageing as the issue of *control* - over the social resources of wealth and knowledge and still over our bodies, degenerating and worthless as they seem to men. (Ritcey, 1982).

Ritcey's comment focuses on one of the most significant themes to emerge during the second group. As in the first group, the leadership issue demonstrated this most strongly but, with the second, factors which we have characterised as the myth of health also proved to be important.

Some group meetings were tape recorded and these recordings show the extent to which leadership issues and in particular issues of power and control featured in the group process. In session one for instance, the leaders hoped to consolidate and differentiate this group from others in Ash House by beginning with introductions. This was rejected as unnecessary by group members as they already knew each other. Seating was always a crucial aspect of the group's process. The downstairs lounge where we held the group meetings was comfortable in some ways but inappropriate in others. Its shape made a circle of chairs difficult to arrange. These linear seating arrangements proved to be a great disadvantage for some members who could not hear or see and were therefore excluded from what was going on. As leaders, we both commented on these disadvantages and failed to persuade members of the group that a circle of chairs would be easier. We have already commented on one aspect of the significance of coming into an environment where alliances and groupings were already established. Existing patterns of leadership within Ash House were replicated in the group. The clearest example of this was the dominance of one member who holds a very prominent position in the tenants' association, who spoke a lot and who tended to organise practical issues and the agenda, frequently without sufficient consultation with other group members. She was the most obvious rival for leadership, but there were others and, in general, the atmosphere in meetings was challenging, particularly in relation to the leaders' integrity and credibility. This atmosphere felt like a continual struggle for control and leadership which conflicted with our attempts to adopt collaborative approaches. Clearly these issues of leadership and power are always around as part of the group process, but the strength of the feelings produced in the Ash House group and in the members and leaders was greater than anticipated.

These complex issues of leadership were compounded by our realisation rather late in the group's process, that the members continued to make links between our power as leaders of the group and the power of the wardens in Ash House.

Initially, in the first two meetings, the group members were positive about the wardens' contribution to the quality of life in Ash House. 'In sheltered housing we have tremendous support from the wardens.....it's marvellous'. '(They) don't interfere until it is absolutely necessary and if you want help they are always there'. However, by the fifth and final meeting, members were more honest about their ambivalent feelings. 'We are always told we must ask the warden'. '(The warden) arranges a lot of things for us here so naturally she is the person that one must go to'.

The very existence of the wardens and any reliance on them, presupposed a degree of dependency and vulnerability which the members of the group fought to resist. The wardens were perceived as having the power of admission to and removal from Ash House, and this power explains some of the ambivalent feelings towards them and to us by proxy.

133

In the social services area office, Ash House has a reputation for housing fit tenants and this was emphasised by the members of the group. They told us that we would get a better response from people living in other housing schemes as they would be less independent and more needy. 'We are not really a fair representation: we are alert and young in mind'. 'I think you make too much of age differences: we are people like everybody else'.

Social workers in the area office have seen an interesting pattern develop over time, whereby mentally and physically vulnerable people were excluded from Ash House. The wardens seemed to respond to increased dependency or frailty by demanding an immediate response from social workers, doctors, police or hospital staff. The group seemed to repeat some of these patterns. For instance, the door was shut on one woman who appeared to have some dementia, and little consideration was given to women with hearing or language difficulties. The group members appeared anxious to perpetuate a myth of healthy, capable and contented tenants: a happy family. In her work, with rheumatoid arthritis sufferers, Wiener (1978) analyses the various strategies of 'keeping up' and 'covering up'. This seemed relevant to our work with these older women because of the uncertainty inherent in their position in both structural and personal terms. When later we came to recognise the anxieties which emerged in the group, a frightening image was seen of tenants who could not admit to vulnerabilities: one of their fears being that to do so would lead to eviction. However, despite this, most members talked of dementia as being a certainty, and so one can imagine their feelings of anxiety and insecurity. The 'myth of health' was therefore very fragile, and clearly our group proved a major threat to its existence for both wardens and tenants. In our view this was a major reason why they were not able to acknowledge the negative aspects of life at Ash House.

View of the group

We began this paper by recognising that involvement with women by workers was a central characteristic of feminist social work. What we feel needs further recognition and discussion are the implications of this approach for the workers involved. Our experience of the second group

134

has shown that far more attention needs to be paid to these boundary issues.

In the first group, we came close to the experience of pain, loss and redundancy that the women felt. With the second group, the experience was different; we were challenged as leaders and our integrity questioned so that after our experience of the second group we felt powerless and inadequate. 'You say we should talk about so and so but what do *you* think, and you look at us all and everybody's mind goes blank'. 'It's all a lot of talk - it all sounds very good but it doesn't come to anything'. 'I think we all feel really that we don't need you'. Ritcey (1982) quotes Simone de Beauvoir: 'They (older women) are "the other" defined as objects, associated with being rather than doing, reluctantly, if ever, awarded the status of subject'.

Gradually, we came to understand, through supervision and working relationships, that these strong opinions and feelings reflected the position of the women in Ash House. By making us feel reified, angry and powerless, they shared with us their feelings about their experience of being older women. The second group therefore seems to have become a microcosm of life in Ash House providing direct insight into the women's worlds. Strong negative feelings were both denied and projected onto others.

Conclusion

On looking back over our groupwork experience, it would seem to fit into Richards' (1987) definition of the primary sphere of social work activity: that of 'developing competencies' rather than one which takes a 'deficit' model which labels the individual group as having problems. The values are for consumer participation, openness of communication, and the concept of mutuality. Fundamental to effective work at this level, is the capacity to 'work alongside' the people one is trying to help. They are not 'clients'. Richards goes on to identify five areas of knowledge and skill which social workers need when embarking on this kind of groupwork. We would suggest an additional necessary skill would be that of explaining the advantages and potential of groupwork for those who do not identify themselves as clients. All too often, social work can be seen by workers and consumers alike as a residual service (Beresford and Croft, 1986), and this reflected the view of the women with whom we worked. When the goals are concerned with raising self esteem and self actualisation rather than with meeting basic needs, the educational approach inherent in Richards' primary sphere demands a long-term commitment.

Some aspects of feminist analysis that we have highlighted in this paper would seem to provide an initial framework for making connections between the personal and the political. We have also identified some areas where leadership and boundaries are particularly central, as is the organisational context in which the groupwork takes place. In spite of some of the difficulties this paper has described, groupwork still remains an attractive alternative. As Donnelly indicates, the progress of this work is erratic and essentially long-term. Our experiences therefore have to be seen as part of an on-going process of developing the practice of groupwork with older women.

11 Types of inter-generational relations: perspectives from Port Talbot

Jackie Lucas

Port Talbot is a coastal town of some 50,000 persons. Until the 1980s, it was accurately described as a steel town, given the sheer number of Port Talbot people who once worked at the plant of the British Steel Corporation. The adjective is now less suitable due to the painful contractions that it has suffered since 1974. However, the steelworks still dominates the eastern end of the town, and the traffic is dreadful at shift changing times. Now, in the later 1980s, it is a town suffering, and attempting to recover, from the massive redundancies of the recession (Harris, 1987). Male unemployment in July 1988 was 14 per cent.

Accompanying the redundancies, came adjustments which led to changes in the population. In the 1950s, thousands moved to the area to work in the steel plant and ancillary industries. Since the mid 1970s more and more young people have left the town, heading for areas where there is a better chance of employment. Between 1981 and 1987 the population of Port Talbot fell from almost 55,000 to 49,000.

One consequence of the migration of mainly young people is a rise in the proportion of elderly people living in the Borough. This has placed strains on families and on the local authorities. Housing provision for the elderly, for example, is one area of concern and suitable housing stock is at a premium. Local housing associations are now building accommodation for this sector of the population, but demand still exceeds supply.

My field research investigated the experience of change in the lives of Port Talbot women, aged between 20 and 40 years. My sample of 300 women was taken from a list of patients in one local general practice. I administered a questionnaire to screen for a high degree of change, particularly over the preceding year, and then conducted semi-structured interviews with the women who qualified. The data in this paper comes mainly from the pilot study undertaken in the spring of 1988, and the remainder is taken from conversations with informants.

Inter-generational relations

Inter-generational relations can be conceived of as being divided into two qualitatively distinct pairs. Firstly, there are relations between same sex members of different generations as against cross-sex relations between members of different generations, and secondly there is assistance flowing from the older generation to the younger as against care and support provided for the elderly. The changing quality and quantity of these inter-generational relations in the sample can be analysed given the breadth and scope of the research.

In this chapter, examples of aid to young people by the older generation and of care of the older generation by the young are described. Conflicts arising from these examples are discussed in relation to three key notions: responsibility, obligation and reciprocity.

Aid to young people

Sussman states that 'the turning to kin when in trouble before using other agencies .... is the mode rather than the exception' (1965, p. 71). This statement was borne out in the situations I found in Port Talbot. My research concerned upheaval, challenge and change, whether for the better or for the worse. Assistance from kin in such circumstances is a

138

significant aspect of my data. A large proportion of these youngish women reported receiving help from their parents, both financial and practical. Sussman (1965, p. 68) concludes from his research that 'while there may be a difference in the absolute amount of financial aid received by families of middle and working class status, there are insignificant differences in the proportion of families in these two strata who report receiving, giving, or exchanging economic assistance in some form'. Rosser and Harris (1965) provide a discussion of this phenomenon in Swansea and reach a similar conclusion.

The following two cases illustrate the extension of economic assistance to children who are well into their adult lives, and represent examples of middle and working class families respectively. (Note that I am using self-perceptions of class throughout in this analysis.)

> Michelle is 32. Her mother is 71, a retired schoolteacher. Michelle had lived away for ten years, and returned to Port Talbot on the break up of her marriage. She has no children. Michelle failed to find employment in the area when she arrived home, and has only worked sporadically on temporary clerical contracts since she returned to Port Talbot in 1985. She lives with her boyfriend in a rented flat. Her mother has helped her financially for the past three years. In particular, she has assisted in paying the deposit on the flat, and has helped in Michelle's attempts to find work by paying for travel outside the area. Michelle has received economic assistance from her mother periodically since her father died in 1976 but, since her marital break up in 1985, the help has increased tremendously. Michelle 'feels bad' about this and experiences a sense of conflict. She believes that, at her age, she should not be 'depending' on her mother and that her mother should be free to enjoy the financial benefits of a teacher's pension without the continual drain of supporting an economically dependent adult offspring. Michelle is the only child and her mother helps her willingly. Her mother's view is that Michelle will reciprocate financially when she can. At the moment she can only help her mother with household chores, particularly cooking, which her mother dislikes. She also assists in arranging for her mother's car to be repaired, for decorators and workmen to call, and takes her mother shopping twice a week.

It is interesting to note that Hill (1970, pp. 69-79) reports from his research that 'the youngest generations .... defined help both given and received as exchange not gifts'. The statement is borne out in Michelle's case and in the following.

139

Richard is 36 and lives with his girlfriend. He has had only temporary or occasional work throughout his adult life but has just obtained permanent work after eight years of unemployment. He lived in London until 1983 when he returned home to Port Talbot due to the expense of living there without work. His mother was widowed in 1975 and is now 65 and retired. She continually helped him out financially whilst he was in London. In recent years she has found it a strain to continue to assist her son in this way. When he came home, she made it clear that any future financial assistance had to be repaid in full when he received his fortnightly giro-cheque. Richard feels indebted to his mother for her support over the years, and has experienced conflict due to it. He redoubled his efforts to find work and, in 1988, having obtained a job, he set up home with his girlfriend. He continues to help his mother with heavy household chores and has cared for her when she has fallen ill over the past five years. However, he now feels that the financial support she has provided has encouraged her to 'interfere' in his life. It is for this reason that he is now keen to be independent of that support. Nonetheless, he accepts that she would still 'help out' if need arises.

Leonard (1980, pp. 64-5), from her study of marriage in Swansea, reports that continuing aid to adult children from the mother 'increases her .... basis for a claim to care in old age'. Michelle's mother admits that her continued financial aid to her daughter is, in a way, in lieu of services she may need from her daughter in the future. In contrast, Richard's mother is of the opinion that one's children will not always reciprocate the help they are given when the parent requires it in old age. 'Claims' are not, therefore, bound to be acknowledged, although the norm exists locally.

A little more can be said about the subjective class experience of the two mothers. Michelle's parents were both schoolteachers. Her mother thinks of herself as middle class and has middle class aspirations for her daughter. She cannot afford to help her daughter financially without 'doing without' herself, but she does not want to 'see her daughter suffer'. She feels responsible for her welfare. Richard's parents were 'well to do' working class, his mother having been a secretary for most of her adult life. His father was a train driver. From the accounts of both Richard and his mother, the household prided itself on a 'working class' attitude and a working class lifestyle. Like Michelle's, Richard's mother could not really afford to help with money, but did so until she retired, when the help was transmuted into loans instead of the gifts of previous years.

140

The third case, that of Christine, is also an example of middle class self-definition.

> Christine is 34, a clerical worker. Her sister lives away, and she remains the only child living near her parents. As her father works away regularly she spends a lot of time with her mother, taking her out during the day. She also invited both parents to stay while their house was being renovated. Christine receives emotional support from her mother which has helped her through a difficult period in her life. Her relationship with her husband deteriorated last year until they were on the verge of a break up. Though her mother's support has been invaluable, aspects of this support have had an ambiguous effect. Christine reports that her mother, having middle class aspirations always disapproved of her marriage, not caring for her husband's family. The emotional support therefore produces a conflict: her mother's attitude reinforces her own insecurity in her marriage, and no doubt compounds the problems in relations with her husband.

The case of Ann illustrates another aspect of help given: the significance of who gives it and who does not.

> Ann, 21, receives no help from her parents at all, despite the fact that she has a young family. Her parents split up when she was 15 and she then lived with both parties in turn, being 'kicked out' of both houses due to violent disagreements. The eldest of a large family, Ann still smarts from her parents' treatment of her. Her husband's family, on the other hand, have been very good to the couple. They provided for their wedding, even though this is traditionally the responsibility of the bride's parents. They live close to the couple, and assist them in many ways. This hurts Ann a little because it is in such contrast to her own parents' lack of support. Ann's parents live some miles away and visit very rarely. Ann has just given birth to her second child, and regrets that her mother has not called to see her since the confinement. Apparently she only contacted Ann 'to find out if it was a girl, because she (the mother) wanted a girl'.

Leonard (1980, p. 48) suggests that "'to leave home" implies a breach with one's parents'. Ann thinks that her breach with her parents stems from the fact that each in turn 'kicked her out'. She did not leave home of her own accord and would not have left at all if it had not been forced upon her. When she had nowhere to go she took a bedsit with help from her boyfriend, whom she later married. She did not enjoy living there, however. Leonard (p. 50) states 'only under major provocation are parents seen to be justified in turning them out of the house'. In Ann's

141

case, neither Ann nor her husband believes there was 'major provocation'. Therefore, Ann does not think her parents' behaviour was 'justified'. According to this norm, Ann concludes that her parents behaved unreasonably. The norm, which Ann accepts, produces a conflict in Ann, as her own situation palpably deviates from it.

In regard to Michelle's case, it might be said that 32-year-old women are usually financially independent of their parents. To Michelle, it was *this* norm that proved a source of tension. Similarly, Richard found the same norm of adult independence from parental economic assistance to be a source of conflict. Although Leonard reports that help to one's children continues into adult life, it was exceptional in my research for this to persist for as long as in the cases of Richard and Michelle, continuing as it did sporadically throughout the early years of adulthood and into their thirties. Also, although kin are culturally expected to help each other out in crises, both Richard and Michelle accepted that their need for help had been too protracted to be 'fair'. They both felt they could 'never pay back' the help they had received. Accordingly, both of them, by accepting these norms, experienced certain conflicts and tension.

Care and support for the elderly

Finch (1987, p. 156) suggests, with reference to the norm of children caring for elderly parents, that 'this norm is of course expressed at a very general level which admits a number of different ways of fulfilling it, and this immediately opens up the possibility of negotiation'. This can be applied to the norm under discussion here. The cases of Richard and Michelle point to the importance of *implicit* negotiations in the kin support arena. The negotiations in these cases were carried out implicitly between the generations.

Reciprocity is a significant element in Michelle's situation, and relevant in Richard's. Michelle expressed her attitude to the help she provides for her mother in terms of reciprocity: 'She helps me out, so I do anything I can to help *her*'. In these examples, a 'balanced' reciprocity seems impossible to the protagonists, although the reciprocal performing of various chores does alleviate some of the tensions experienced. Following Sahlins (1965), 'generalised' reciprocity pertains which demands a less immediate return of services provided.

Regarding the situation in South Wales, it has been reported that the 'claim to care in old age' was 'basically fulfilled in Swansea' (Leonard, 1980, pp. 64-5). This research result is confirmed by Harris' conclusions (Harris, 1975), and is supported by my research in Port Talbot.

> Catherine, 30, lives with her boyfriend and her two children from a previous relationship, and her grandfather. She is one of several children and says 'there's no room at my mother's' for the grandfather. Her grandfather came to live with her when he attempted suicide. Despite being in the throes of relationship problems at the time, Catherine 'wouldn't let him go home' because 'his wife treats him badly', and persuaded him to move in with her and her family. She enjoys her grandfather staying with her. He is in good health, and gets on very well with the children, and they with him.

Michelle and Richard, as discussed above, help their elderly mothers with household tasks. Michelle takes her mother shopping, cooks frequently for her, and arranges household repairs. Richard visits his mother three times a week, walks her large dog, and mows the sizeable garden. Another case, that of Grace and Cheryl, illustrates a different set of circumstances.

> Grace and Cheryl, a mother aged 63 and a daughter aged 40, live in Port Talbot in separate households. Their family has lived in the town for thirty years, but still keeps in frequent contact with close relatives who live in their home town of Pontardawe. In particular, Cheryl and Grace travel there weekly to visit Cheryl's grandmother, Grace's mother-in-law, who is over 90 and lives alone. Although this older woman has closer relatives nearby, both Cheryl and Grace worry that she is not being cared for adequately by those who live near. Cheryl decorates her house when necessary, and Grace provides various services for her. Both Cheryl and Grace invite her to stay regularly, Grace entertaining her at Christmas every year. Grace's mother-in-law enjoys fairly good health, but can be difficult when she comes to stay. When she returns home, Grace is usually relieved. Grace visits her mother-in-law because she feels 'responsible' for her. She basically regards visiting to be a necessity, as she is concerned for her mother-in-law's welfare. Grace has an old car and can barely afford to run it now she has retired. She worries about what will happen to her mother-in-law when the car is gone and she cannot visit so regularly. Grace has a busy life and runs several church organisations. She also has to help her daughter with household chores as Cheryl suffers from a chronic complaint that can sometimes incapacitate her. Grace rarely complains

about visiting her mother-in-law despite her other commitments. She enjoys the visits, which enable her to keep in touch with other relatives in her home town. However, the frequent visits are hard for her to maintain. Also, she is well aware that as a daughter-in-law she does a great deal for her mother-in-law that the latter's children do not attend to. She believes that they *should* provide more help than they do. However, even though her husband is dead, she sees no anomaly in her continued kindness to her mother-in-law, as she feels that it is needed.

Finch (1987, p. 158) discusses family obligations and the norms governing the care of elderly people, stating 'the very fact that the norms themselves are frequently expressed in very generalised terms which need to be applied to specific situations almost requires an element of negotiation'. Grace's experience does not illustrate the negotiation aspect well. The cases of Michelle and Richard, demonstrating situations where help is given by elderly parents to adult children, seem to illustrate this point more adequately. The negotiations involved in Michelle's case I would suggest are implicit.

Sussman (1965, p. 70) states that 'services to old persons .... are expected and practiced roles of children and other kin members. These acts of filial and kin responsibility are performed voluntarily without law or compulsion'. This statement runs at a tangent somewhat to Leonard (1980, pp. 64-5) when she states that a mother's aid to married children 'increases her .... basis for a claim to care in old age'. The latter notion emphasises the reciprocal nature of kin relations; the former stresses the element of social compulsion that is involved. Although Sussman underlines the voluntary nature of such actions, he nevertheless accentuates that such behaviour is 'expected'.

However, the *quantity* and *quality* of services 'expected' is not normatively regulated. Although some of my informants complained bitterly of the lack of filial or parental devotion by some, or praised the assiduous attention paid to an elderly relative by others, there is no real norm governing what is expected of kin when it comes to 'helping out' their families. Such help is rendered on an ad hoc basis. Sense tells people if they or others are doing too much or too little. However, judgements regarding individuals are made on the performance of such tasks. The norm of caring for elderly people, like that of assisting one's adult children, is important to those I interviewed.

144

Three kinds of conflict arise in the inter-generational relations that have been examined. The first are conflicts due to situations differing from norms. Into this category fall those conflicts experienced by Michelle and Richard because of lengthy financial support from their parents, and those felt by Ann, due to the lack of help from her parents contrasted with assiduous support from her in-laws.

The case of Grace could also be included here, as her situation as daughter-in-law is ambivalent. It could be said that it is not culturally expected that a daughter-in-law should help out her mother-in-law extensively once her husband has died, especially in a situation where other closer kin are in a better position to assist.

Grace's case also illustrates the second kind of conflict: that arising from overload. Grace is busy and must fit visits to her mother-in-law into a full schedule. Similarly Catherine's situation could *develop* into overload given a crisis or a change in the circumstances of her grandfather. Regarding aid from the older generation, the mothers of Richard and Michelle could also be said to have experienced *financial* overload, in the sense of a burden which led to a conflict between their desire to assist their children and their expectations for their own standards of living. Both women are pensioners with extremely limited resources.

The third type of conflict demonstrated, is that due to certain effects of kin support. The assistance given may constitute, or may lead to, interference in the life of the person in receipt of help. This holds true in Richard's case. Christine's case could be said to illustrate this also, in the sense that her mother's disapproval of her husband 'interferes' with her own relationship with him.

Discussion

As I have shown, the norms of caring for elderly people and of assisting one's adult children are important in the ways in which people describe their family relationships. Such norms create 'idioms' for expressing displeasure or satisfaction with the behaviour of others. I use the word 'idiom' because such expressions convey ways of talking about these kinds of issues. It helps in the analysis of how people talk about responsibility, obligation and reciprocity. As responsibility and reciprocity are not regulated in any formal way through rules of behaviour, these idioms also express many of the problems, conflicts and tensions inherent in certain types of inter-generational relations.

Arising out of this study is evidence of the cultural significance of two idioms involved in the giving and receiving of help between the generations. These are obligation (and the associated responsibility) and reciprocity. The first seems to express both motivations for action and the effects of some aspects of the help either given or received. The second underlies action and motivations in some cases, but only emerges as a truly significant idiom in the cases of Michelle and Richard. Both find the idiom of reciprocity helpful in diminishing the conflicts that they experience. Their mothers, in their eyes, have long ceased to be responsible for them. In this context, receipt of continued help which they are unable to reciprocate fully, generates feelings of obligation. However, the services they perform for their mothers alleviate the conflicts experienced.

The norms of parental responsibility towards children, and of filial responsibility towards the elderly, seem to create conflict when the situation does not conform to the norm, or to the idioms through which this norm is expressed. Michelle says 'I feel bad as I'm 32 years old and my mother still buys my clothes'. Grace, however willingly she helps her mother-in-law, is resentful of the fact that there are closer relatives in a position to provide much more assistance than they do. Moreover, she feels it is their responsibility to assist, not hers. How then might different idioms help to reduce the sense of grievance that can arise within families?

If the idiom of reciprocity were more significant in these examples, one might find some conflicts avoided, or at least, diverted. An idiom which states 'I help her now because she was good to me in the past' might be easier to accommodate than one which states 'I'm responsible for her: I *must* help her out'. The idiom of reciprocity could be seen to include a notion of balance, thus helping to regulate how much one should do for someone and how much one should expect from the same person. This contrasts with the idiom of diffuse obligation arising from imbalances in the exchanges of a particular pair. In this case, there are no norms defining the nature of the obligation and, accordingly, one never knows if one is doing too much or too little.

Certain behaviours are culturally expected of kin when relatives are in trouble or when they need continuous help for some reason. However, no rules govern these behaviours. Idioms of obligation and responsibility let people know what they *should* do, but nothing tells them what they *must* do. Therefore, problems can arise for both the helper and the helped. The quality of support received can be a problem: the idea of 'creating a burden' may produce conflict for the helped (see McKee, 1987).

Reciprocity remains however, in such a situation, as a subsidiary idiom: 'After all she's done for me, the least I can do is . . . '. On the basis of my research I would suggest that an idiom of reciprocity can ease the situation for the helper and for those who receive support, given suitable circumstances. One could conclude by suggesting that the idiom of reciprocity has as much practical significance in regard to inter-generational relations, if not more, than the idioms of obligation and responsibility.

12 Fifty years on: elderly people in London and Britain

Jane Falkingham and Chris Gordon

The last decade has seen increasing interest in the issue of the respective roles of the family and the community in helping elderly people in need. Partly this is one particular expression of a political ideology which elevates self-help and the role of the individual as against 'intrusion' by the state. However, it also reflects recent and projected demographic experience and in particular the growth in the proportion of elderly people in the population, from 6 per cent in 1901 to 18 per cent at the last census (DHSS, 1984).

The cost of providing resources for such growing numbers of elderly people has prompted a re-evaluation of the role of the state in that provision. Past times have been used to justify a 'return' to individual responsibility, self-help, and for a withdrawal of the collectivity. In particular, as Thomson notes, 'the experiences of the Victorian era ... have been cited on many occasions in support of a drive to make individuals more responsible for the welfare of themselves and their relatives' (Thomson, 1986, p. 355). There is a presumption today that families in past times were willing to take on this responsibility. This is a presumption which would have surprised most Victorian families

(Thomson, 1986) and working class families in London in the 1930s (Gordon, 1988). Yet, when the Green Paper on the Reform of Social Security highlighted the importance of 'personal provision' and when, for instance, the White Paper *Growing Older* stressed the primary importance of informal care for the elderly and the personal ties of kinship and friendship, implicit was a presumed historical experience which justified less of a role for the state (DHSS, 1985, para. 1.5, and DHSS, 1981, para. 1.9). This assumption was reiterated in the Griffiths Report (1988) and more recently in the White Paper *Caring for People* (DoH, 1989).

The reasons why such an approach continues to be maintained, and why a re-emphasis on the role of the family, apart from being unjustified by historical evidence, may be in itself highly inappropriate today have been discussed elsewhere (Gordon, 1988, p. 288-291). This chapter comments on changes over the last fifty years in the relative importance of the family and the state, focusing on two particular features of old age - the co-residential experience of the elderly and their sources of income.

Co-resident kin have been identified as an important source of assistance for elderly relatives in present times (Evandrou et al, 1986). It is important, therefore, to consider co-residence in the past as a means of support and the extent to which co-residence patterns have changed over time. This may suggest the limits to which co-residence can be relied upon. A comparison of household structure over time also allows one to look at certain effects of social, economic and demographic changes: the fall in family size, changes in labour force participation, and the emergence of a well-heeled gerontocracy within the ranks of the elderly. These too may suggest the extent to which calls for greater family responsibility are even appropriate. Similarly, comparing income by source may reveal the consistent reliance of the elderly on the state for the bulk of their income, the extent to which the composition of sources has shifted over time, and how incomes have compared with the poverty line and the wealth of the nation.

Methodology: *historical sources*

Investigations of long-term trends in the demographic and economic characteristics of Britain are severely hampered by the sparsity of published information prior to the 1950s. The first census took place in

1801 and from that, and subsequent censuses, only very basic demographic data about elderly people can be obtained: age distributions, marital status, and labour force participation rates. A question on household composition was included from 1851, but, except for 1851, it was not until the 1951 census that the information collected was actually published. Ironically, therefore, we are in the curious position of knowing much more about the household characteristics of the elderly for periods prior to 1861 - through family reconstitutions based on parish registers - than we are for the following century. It is possible, as Anderson and Armstrong have demonstrated, to use the original enumerators' returns to retrieve such information, for example, for Preston in 1841 and for York in 1841 and 1851 (Anderson, 1971, and Armstrong, 1972). This approach is not possible, however, with later unpublished census data as the 'hundred year closure' rule restricts access after 1881, although some household composition data from the censuses of 1891-1921 for several small communities has been analysed (Wall et al, 1988).

Data on the incomes of elderly people are readily available for the last thirty years or so (see Fiegehen, 1986, for instance). Furthermore, a plethora of unofficial social surveys before the Second World War, concerned to demonstrate the existence and extent of poverty, collected data on the income of specific groups of the elderly for earlier times (see Gordon, 1988, p. 292). However, these did not produce much information on the *sources* of income received.

It becomes very difficult then to compare, for example, the household structure and sources of income of elderly people during the course of this century. There is, however, one inter-war social survey, the New Survey of London (NSOL) (Llewellyn Smith, 1930-34), which allows us to study these characteristics for elderly people in the early 1930s, and thereby enables us to make a comparison across a period of fifty years. The NSOL was the most significant, and by far the largest, unofficial social survey of its time. It covered 28,100 working class households and included 98,400 people. It was intended as a follow-up to Booth's monumental survey of London's working class (Booth, 1892-97) and is, therefore, predominantly a poverty study itself. The survey collected data on elderly people's income by source, along with some extremely useful and rarely exploited incidental data, including household composition. The original data cards from this survey have been preserved, and it is likely to be the only major source of this kind of information for the early 1930s. The 1931 census returns, for example, were destroyed by fire in 1942, and the next census was not until 1951.

The NSOL was a survey of the working class in London, and was carried out between 1928 and 1930. In this chapter, a subsample consisting of all those boroughs within the London County Council area north of the Thames is used. This includes nearly 2,300 elderly people distributed across 1,900 households. The results of an earlier analysis of this data have been published in Gordon (1988). What clearly emerged were the high rates of solitary living by elderly people, their high headship rates, and that co-residence with children was far from being the norm among the working class of the early 1930s. That analysis also demonstrated how little the elderly depended on direct cash assistance from kin outside the household unit, a finding which echoes that of Thomson (1986).

It is possible to use the NSOL data in conjunction with roughly equivalent data from the 1979-81 General Household Surveys (GHSs) to provide a long-run picture[1]. Although the analysis is limited to only two points in time, it gives some indication of long-term trends and suggests hypotheses that can be tested. Three years of the GHS were pooled to provide the 1979-81 data set. As well as covering the same time span as did the NSOL, the use of three years of the GHS also overcomes the problem of having low cell counts at disaggregated levels. These GHSs each provide nationally representative samples of around 30,000 individuals, which in turn provided a pooled subsample for the three years of some 13,600 people aged 65 years and over living in private households in Great Britain. Of these, 1,690 were living in London, of whom 945 were classified as working class.

Methodology: *the NSOL and the GHS - problems of equivalence*

There are always difficulties with this approach of comparing different data sets over time. The most obvious problem here is that of achieving

---

[1]   Because the income section of the GHS questionnaire was radically revised in 1979, data for 1978, which would have permitted a comparison over exactly fifty years, were not directly comparable with those for later years. Thus the GHS years used were 1979-81.

151

geographical equivalence. The data for 1928-30 are based on the London County Council boroughs north of the Thames, while those from the 1979-81 GHSs relate to all the boroughs within the former Greater London Council area. Nothing can be done about this since further regional disaggregation for the GHS is not possible. However, it is unlikely that the inclusion of south London in the GHS data set will cause any major bias in the comparisons.

More problematic perhaps is the choice of criteria for selecting the 'working class' subsample for 1979-81 with which to compare that of 1928-30. Occupation rather than income was the main determinant of class status in the NSOL (Llewellyn Smith, 1930-34, v. 6, p. 149-153). In some cases, however, 'any card relating to a house of obviously "middle class" grade was ... rejected irrespective of occupation' (ibid, v. 6, p. 153). Manual workers, whether unskilled or not, were classified as working class, and non-manual workers generally as middle class. A few exceptions were noted, for example, shop owners and shop assistants, and the self employed if their incomes were definitely below £250 p.a. were considered working class (ibid, v. 3, p. 416). The classification was based on the occupation of the father, or of the principal wage earner. Thus, even if the children of manual wage earners were employed in non-manual occupations, the whole family was classed with the father (ibid, v. 3, p. 35). Such a description actually admits of a certain ambiguity. How were the elderly heads of households treated? What if a middle class child was the principal wage earner, or if a household lacked a father and a wage earner? It seems that what the classification was designed to do was to identify working class *households* as opposed to working class *individuals*. There can have been no absolute consistency about which individual in the household defined the social characteristics of that household. It need not apparently have been the head of that household, though almost invariably it would have been. By modern survey standards these definitions are lamentably unrigorous. To match the NSOL it was decided to select a sample from the GHS data using HOHCLASS, the social class of the head of the household. In theory the sample will include 'non-working class elderly' living in households where the household head is classified as working class. Similarly it will exclude the working-class elderly living in non-working class households. This presumably is what happened in the NSOL, so not all the working-class

152

elderly would have been included in its working class sample. For a more detailed account of the selection of the sample, the reader is directed to Falkingham and Gordon (1988).

Classes IIIM, IV and V (skilled manual, semi-skilled and unskilled occupations) in the GHS were combined and taken to approximate to the NSOL's working class. This is not entirely satisfactory since social and occupational changes across those fifty years have undoubtedly been significant. The growth of the white collar sector, for example, has been an important feature. One illustration of these changes is provided by the fact that the NSOL estimated the working class to account for almost 72 per cent of London's workers (ibid, v. 6, p. 152). However, in the 1979-81 GHSs, classes IIIM, IV and V accounted for only 46 per cent of London's adult population. Nevertheless, our approach will allow some broad indication of change over time which owes only a little, if anything at all, to these methodological difficulties.

Analysis

Headship of households

Headship rates provide a measure 'of the extent to which the elderly retain the various responsibilities usually associated with the running of a distinct residential and consumption unit' (Wall, 1989, p. 125). The significance of this measure lies in the presumption that heading a household indicates a form of independence. The definition of household head used by the NSOL, and by the GHS, makes it possible for a married woman to head a household only if her husband is absent.

According to the NSOL, in the late 1920s, over 90 per cent of elderly working class men and 57 per cent of working class women in London were household heads. Such a high rate for women is somewhat surprising given the definitional restriction. Whereas headship rates for men declined a little with increasing age, for women they rose significantly. Although men may have been moving into the households of younger relatives in later years, most of this pattern is probably accounted for by the definition of household head and by the differential life expectations of men and women.

153

What emerges most strikingly from the comparison between the NSOL and the GHSs is the close similarity of the patterns pertaining in 1928-30 and in 1979-81 (Table 12-1). It is surprising that headship rates for the elderly as a whole have not increased, even among women. The fall in family sizes might have been expected to bring about earlier and more frequent solitary living and the fall in the age of marriage between 1945 and 1968 might have led children to leave the parental home at an earlier age. Furthermore, other factors might have encouraged the growth of headship rates: rising real incomes, for instance, would have made independent home ownership more possible.

Table 12-1 *Percentage of London working-class elderly people reported to be heads of households by age, gender and period*

	Males 1928-30	1979-81	Females 1928-30	1979-81
65-69	95	96	51	44
70-74	93	95	52	60
75-79	88	91	67	66
80+	82	85	74	77
65+	92	94	57	59
Total (= 100%)	930	395	1354	550

Further light is shed on trends in headship by examining the data published in the 1951 census, and reproduced in Table 12-2 (GRO, 1952). It is clear from this that, both at the national level and in London, headship rates among the elderly have risen over the last thirty years. This suggests that there was a fall somewhere between the 1930s and the 1950s, and a rise thereafter to levels largely similar to those of 1928-30. If so, this may have followed a period of relative stability: the analysis of a sample from the 1891-1921 censuses show a remarkable similarity in headship rates over those four decades, albeit across only a few communities (Wall et al, 1988). These rates are also very similar to those calculated for a collection of communities in 'pre-industrial' England by Laslett (1977).

Table 12-2 *Percentage of all elderly people reported as head of household, by gender*

	Males	Females	All	Total (= 100%)
1599–1796*	88	39	62	(562)
1891	84	39	60	(1702)
1901	84	37	58	(1678)
1911	83	36	58	(1964)
1921	84	40	60	(2491)
1951 G.B.*	84	37	57	(7.7m)
1980 G.B.*	95	48	68	(6250)
1951 London*	85	43	60	(0.54m)
1980 London*	97	53	71	(769)

* Refers to those over 60 years of age.

Sources: 1599-1796 - Laslett (1977, p. 201)
1891-1921 - Wall et al (1988, Table 3)
1951   - GRO (1952, Tables I.1 and V.1)
1980   - General Household Survey (1982)

Falkingham and Gordon (1988, table A.1) show how the GHS rates vary by class and region. The working-class elderly have slightly higher headship rates than the elderly as a whole, and London's elderly have higher headship rates than the elderly nationally, a feature which also emerged from the 1951 census. The pattern of higher headship rates for the working class is also evident in London, and leads to what might be termed a 'London effect'. What this suggests in explaining variations in headship rates, at least among the elderly, is that selecting on region may be just as important as selecting on class.

Living alone

Table 12-3 shows that the proportion of London's working-class elderly who live alone has grown significantly over time. Of London's working-class elderly, 30 per cent lived alone in 1928-30 and this rose to 37 per cent in 1979-81. Among those aged over 75 years, the rise has been even greater, from 44 to 57 per cent. For men under 80 years, the

Table 12-3 *Percentage of London working-class elderly people living alone by age, gender and period*

	Males 1928-30	1979-81	Females 1928-30	1979-81
65-69	13	13	31	33
70-74	20	23	36	52
75-79	26	26	44	56
80+	32	39	50	63
65+	19	21	37	48
Total (= 100%)	930	395	1354	550

proportions by age group are largely the same in 1979-81 as in 1928-30, a characteristic which mirrors the almost unchanged headship rate. Conversely, for women aged over 70 years, the increase over time has been quite marked. Recent GHSs show a similar trend towards living alone over the years 1975-85. Women, not surprisingly, given their lower mortality rates, are more likely to be living alone than men, and the differences between their respective circumstances have increased over time.

Again, London's working-class elderly in 1979-81 have household characteristics which make them a distinct social group (Falkingham and Gordon, 1988, Table A.2). Neither the working-class elderly generally, nor the elderly as a whole, experienced such high rates of headship and solitariness.

A longer-term picture is obtained in Table 12-4 by drawing on data assembled by Laslett (1977), Wall et al (1988), and Shanas et al (1968). This shows firstly, that there are higher rates of living alone for women: a consistent feature of all studies of household composition. Secondly, rates have increased quite markedly over the last three decades but, as we have found from the NSOL, they were already very high among the working class of London in 1930. This suggests the hypothesis that these rates may have fluctuated over time throughout the country but within an underlying trend which was upwards. One caveat to this hypothesis however is suggested by the experience of Bethnal Green. In 1928-30, 26 per cent of

Table 12-4 *Percentage of all elderly people living alone, by gender*

	Males	Females	All	Total (= 100%)
1684-1796	6	14	10	(297)
1891	10	16	13	(514)
1901	7	13	10	(463)
1911	8	9	9	(566)
1921	10	18	14	(596)
1951	8	16	13	(7.7m)
1962*	11	30	22	(2500)
1980*	14	38	28	(6250)

* Refers to those over 60 years of age

Sources: 1684-1796 - those over 65 in five places: Chilvers Coton, 1684; Lichfield, 1695; Stoke-on-Trent, 1701; Corfe Castle, 1790; and Ardleigh, 1796 (Laslett, 1977, Table 5.12)

1891-1921 - based on two communities: Bolton and Morland (Wall et al, 1988, Table 8)

1951 - Great Britain (GRO, 1952, Tables I.1 and V.1)

1962 - Great Britain (Shanas et al, 1968, Table VI-12, and Laslett, 1977, Table 5.12)

1980 - Great Britain (General Household Survey, 1982)

its elderly inhabitants lived alone. Townsend (1963), undertaking a survey of the same borough in the mid 1950s, a time when according to the hypothesis headship rates and rates of solitariness would be comparatively low, found almost exactly the same proportion: 25 per cent.

This suggests an alternative hypothesis: that London has had much higher rates of living alone than the country as a whole from at least the 1920s. Instead of a fluctuating trend one can argue that change has been largely linear and sustained, but that nationally such rapid change did not occur until after 1950. This would be consistent with the levels of solitariness and headship rates reported in the 1951 Census which seem more akin to those for some nineteenth-century communities than those for the last two decades.

Either way, the idea of support from co-residents has to take account of the fact that many of the elderly, particularly the very elderly, simply do not have, nor have they had, co-residents, and that over time they have had them less often. In 1979-81, over a half of all those over the age of 80 years lived alone. What is more, the number of co-residents has fallen over time.

Household size and other household members

In 1928-30, 73 per cent of elderly people were living alone or with one other person. As age increased the tendency to live in small households increased. In 1979-81, nearly 90 per cent of London's working-class elderly lived alone or with only one other person. Again, household sizes tended to decrease across age (Table 12-5). What emerges then is a tendency towards a concentration of elderly people in small households as age increases and over time. It is possible that the decline in the household size of the elderly is part of a longer-term phenomenon dating from the turn of this century, one mirroring the decline in mean household size for all ages.

Table 12-5 *Household size of elderly persons by age and period (percentages)*

	65–69		70–74		75–79		80+	
	1928 –30	1979 –81	1928 –30	1979 –81	1928 –30	1979 –81	1928 –30	1979 –81
1	23	24	30	37	36	45	44	57
2	43	58	46	54	41	43	32	31
3	17	15	14	6	10	6	11	8
4	8	2	5	1	5	0	6	2
5+	9	2	5	2	8	6	7	2
Total (= 100%)	887	351	728	265	336	182	212	147

In 1979-81, London's working-class elderly had household sizes lower than the working class as a whole. More lived alone and more headed their own household. This is surprising, given the relatively higher cost of accommodation in London which might have led one to predict greater

158

co-residence, fewer solitaries and larger household sizes. One possible reason for this paradox is the greater importance of public sector housing provision in London which has provided artifically low housing costs and thereby offset, to some extent, the pressures to co-reside.

Examining the extent to which an elderly person lives in the household of someone of a younger generation, it is evident that this is a rare and declining phenomenon. In 1928-30, the figure was only 9 per cent and, in 1979-81, at most 5.7 per cent - neither impressively large figures. Almost universally then, elderly people either head their own household or are married to those that do. This is true for 1928-30, and for 1979-81, both in London and in Britain as a whole. It was almost as true in Laslett's six pre-industrial communities too, where around 85 per cent of the elderly headed a household or lived with a spouse who did (Laslett, 1977, p. 20). Likewise, Wall's analyses reveal a corresponding figure of around 80 per cent for the years 1891-1921 (Wall et al, 1988, Table 3).

There is also some evidence available from the NSOL on the composition of households lived in by the elderly. Table 12-6 shows that 60 per cent of such households consisted of people living alone or married couples only. The survey forms show that, at most, a third of the elderly lived with a child, that significantly more men did so than women and that, when women lived with a child, it was more often as a lone parent, without the support of a husband (Falkingham and Gordon, 1988, p. 30).

What is also clear from Table 12-6 is that the proportion of households containing members other than a spouse has diminished over the last fifty years from 40 per cent to just over 20 per cent. It is highly unlikely that households containing 'children' will account for the entire 20 per cent in 1979-81. We can reasonably conclude therefore that the period after 1930 has seen a sharp fall in the proportion of the elderly who live with their children.

These analyses have demonstrated the very high headship rates of London's elderly. It is the similarity rather than the growth of these rates which is apparent. Rates of solitariness have grown markedly, however, and household sizes fallen correspondingly. Furthermore, households have tended to consist less and less of members beyond the marital or solitary unit. A longer-term picture leads one to suggest that prior to the twentieth century all these rates may have shown a remarkable degree of stability. It is possible that during the present century there has been at

159

Table 12-6 *Composition of London working class households by gender and period (percentages)*

	Males 1928–30	1979–81	Females 1928–30	1979–81
Single person alone	19	21	37	48
Couple alone	41	56	22	30
Other	40	23	41	22
Total (= 100%)	930	395	1354	550

least one period when national rates of headship and solitariness contracted. Possible explanations for this could be the retrenchment in the housebuilding programme which accompanied the Second World War, and the rise in the birth rate in the mid-1940s. Both would have tended to prolong the period of co-residence. Alternatively, rather than national fluctuations over time, it may be regional variations which have predominated. One might conclude that London's experience has been unique. If there has been rapid change over the last thirty or forty years with co-residence in particular occurring less frequently and for shorter durations, then this may have occurred in London much earlier than elsewhere.

What we should bear in mind, lest we fall into the trap that others have of looking nostalgically (or strategically) back to the last century, is that co-residence of the elderly with kin was far from the norm then, and that they generally operated independent households, even to the point of living alone. The idea then that the co-residential unit could and can therefore be viewed as a strategic component in any consideration of the provision of support for the elderly needs rethinking. The move towards greater residential isolation is by now quite entrenched. But even if it were to be reversed, the co-residential experience of the elderly would be scarcely sufficient to warrant modification of other pillars of support.

Changes in income

Sources of income

From the responses to questions asked in the NSOL and in the GHSs about sources of income, it is possible to look at how the composition of elderly people's income has changed over the past fifty years. Table 12-7 presents the relevant data.

State originated cash benefits emerge as the most frequent source of income for London's elderly both in 1928-30 and in more recent times. Almost all were in receipt of National Insurance pensions in 1979-81 and, given that those not in receipt of a state pension almost invariably received supplementary benefit, income from the state touched virtually every elderly person. This remains the case, whatever level of disaggregation is chosen: the proportion of London's working-class elderly in receipt of an old age pension is almost exactly the same as the proportion of the elderly nationally and of all London's elderly.

Despite being the most important source of income for elderly people in 1928-30, universal receipt of state benefits was far from being achieved. As many as a fifth claimed to be living without any form of state support. One reason for this is that a few, even of the working class, declined to take up the benefit to which they were entitled. Far more important though is the fact that not all elderly persons were eligible for state pensions. Under the terms of the Old Age Pensions Acts 1908-24, a means-tested payment could be claimed by those over 70 years, and under the Widow's, Orphans', and Old Age Contributory Pensions Acts 1925-31, those retiring at 65 years, who had been part of the contributory scheme for two years, were similarly eligible to draw a pension. The result is that, while nearly all those over 70 years were eligible for a pension, not all those aged 65-69 years were. Not everyone was in an insurable occupation or, particularly in the case of women, in any occupation at all. This is the reason for the steep age gradient in 1928-30: only 59 per cent of those aged 65-69 years were in receipt of a pension whereas 89 per cent of those aged 70-74 years were.

Supplementary Benefit (SB) was a means-tested payment (now known as Income Support) designed to bring people out of poverty. Such a benefit did not exist in the 1930s, but the pattern of receipt in the 1980s

161

Table 12-7 *Percentage of London working-class elderly people in receipt of income from different sources, by age, gender and period*

	65-69	70-74	75-79	80+	65+
1928-30 males					
State Benefits	64	90	92	93	80
Employment	49	27	10	(4)	32
Subletting	29	21	30	20	26
Family	(2)	(4)	(10)	(15)	5
Other	9	13	24	(14)	13
Total (= 100%)	390	290	144	74	930
1979-81 males					
NI pension	90	99	98	95	95
SB	19	20	(14)	(13)	22
Employment	24	15	(12)	(0)	17
Occ. pensions	53	50	44	49	50
Savings	48	38	39	(29)	41
Other	(1)	(2)	(3)	(0)	6
Total (= 100%)	160	129	65	41	395
1928-30 females					
State Benefits	55	88	93	96	78
Employment	19	8	(2)	(1)	11
Subletting	14	9	13	10	12
Family	7	7	10	12	9
Other	4	10	9	(10)	18
Total (= 100%)	497	438	192	138	1354
1979-81 females					
NI pension	93	95	98	93	94
SB	21	36	45	61	37
Employment	12	(17)	(2)	(0)	6
Occ. pensions	15	14	20	(7)	14
Savings	38	36	31	25	34
Other	(1)	(1)	(1)	(1)	4
Total (= 100%)	191	136	117	106	550

Note: brackets indicate percentage values based upon small numbers

merits some comment.   The working class in 1979-81 drew more
frequently on it than the elderly as a whole; elderly people in London, and
in particular those in the working classes, more often than other groups
(Falkingham and Gordon, 1988). Within this pattern there are consistent
age and gender differences reflecting the greater incidence of poverty
among women and among the very elderly. In London, nearly two-fifths of
elderly working-class women were in receipt of SB, and among those over
80 years it was three-fifths.

In 1928-30 it was common for elderly men to be in some form of paid
employment: one third of elderly men, compared with one tenth of elderly
women. Employment for both men and women declined markedly with
age. By 1979-81 the importance of employment as a source of income had
diminished. The conditions attached to the receipt of a state pension are
one cause of this phenomenon. Any income from employment now leads
to an almost equivalent fall in the level of state pension received. The
decline of employment as an income source has been almost entirely a
male phenomenon, given the low rates of elderly female labour-force
participation at both points in time. Class status does not seem to have
had any influence on the propensity of the elderly in the 1979-81 sample to
have been in work. Geographical location, however, does: London's
elderly people, in whatever social class, were more likely to have been
engaged in some form of employment than the elderly as a whole, though
the differences are not great.

Subletting accommodation was another common source of income in
1928-30, especially for elderly men. The percentage subletting across age
shows a curious pattern though. Perhaps eligibility for a state pension at
70 years of age accounts in part for the lower percentage of 70-74 year olds
subletting than those in age groups above and below. By 1979-81,
however, subletting as a source of income was largely irrelevant: the
figures, not given here, suggest that at most about 1 per cent of London's
working-class elderly people sublet.

Very few elderly people in 1928-30 claimed to be in receipt of income
from members of the family living outside the household. More women
than men benefited as did those over 75 years of age, but even among this
group only about one in ten were being helped in this way. Direct cash
assistance was uncommon in the early 1930s, but by the early 1980s it was
virtually extinct: the category 'other income' in the GHSs includes income

from the family amongst its sources, and characterises only ten out of 889 cases.

More important to most elderly people in 1928-30 was income from property, occupational pensions and savings rather than from families, at least in terms of numbers in receipt. Women benefited less frequently than men in this way, the reverse to the case of income from families. By 1979-81 the importance of occupational pensions and savings had grown enormously and had become one of the most common sources of non-state income. Occupational pensions were, however, largely male preserves, and many women in receipt of an occupational pension were so, only by virtue of the death of their husbands. Occupational pensions were also more commonly received by the non-working class elderly and by those under 75 years of age. These age patterns reflecting the institutional growth of occupational pensions over the last decade or so, and are identical to those observed for 'savings'. Interestingly, however, the gender differences for savings were not so marked, whereas the class differences were more so. Declining access to income from occupational pensions and savings at higher ages in part accounts for a greater reliance on SB at these ages. In the case of savings, for example, declining receipt across age probably reflects a running down of financial assets, and a corresponding increase in the numbers eligible for SB.

In summary, comparing London's working-class elderly in 1928-30 with those fifty years later, reveals a fairly clear pattern: a marked shift in the percentage drawing on income from employment and subletting to income from the state and, in particular, from occupational pensions and savings. At neither point in time can the importance of the family in financial provision be said to be anything other than residual.

Something can also be said about the distinctiveness of London's elderly, at least for 1979-81. It is apparent that, whether working class or not, they were more likely to draw on employment and SB as sources of income. Indeed, in the case of the former, the effect of selecting on region was greater than of selecting on class. For SB, occupational pensions and savings, however, class rather than region had the greater influence on numbers in receipt.

164

Size of income

So far we have considered the frequency of receipt of income from different sources, but this tells us nothing about the actual values of these income sources. Table 12-8 therefore presents the median values[2], both in regard to particular sources (ignoring those not in receipt) and to total income.

In 1928-30 elderly men had much higher incomes than women, and the younger elderly had higher incomes than those over the age of 75 years. For elderly couples, however, the income of women has become an increasingly significant part of their joint income. Data for 1979-81 suggest that there is now considerably more equality between genders and age groups than fifty years ago. Although elderly men still have higher incomes than women, and the younger men have incomes higher than the cohorts which preceded them, the relative incomes of men and women tend to converge with age. This is characteristic not only of London's working-class elderly, but of the elderly nationally, and of all working-class elderly people.

The incomes of the working-class elderly are less than those of the elderly as a whole, though the differences are scarcely significant for women, and decline over age for men. There is, therefore, a convergence of class experiences across age groups and, once again, it is region rather than class which has the greatest effect on income levels. London's working-class elderly have higher than all elderly, and the highest median incomes are those for the London elderly as a whole. This 'London effect' is characteristic of both genders, and holds for all age groups. One reason is the greater participation of older people in the labour force in London, but it may also have something to do with higher occupational pensions (as a result of higher London wages) and higher receipts from SB to account for higher housing costs in the capital.

In 1928-30 the median income from the state for those in receipt of state benefits was ten shillings, regardless of age or gender; and the standard deviations were quite small. That is not surprising since ten shillings was the standard level of the old age pension. By 1979-81, men

2   In Table 12-8 we restrict ourselves to presenting the data for London's working-class elderly. Tables A6.ii to A6.vii in Falkingham and Gordon (1988) give a more extensive account of median incomes, covering the aggregate national and working class experience.

165

Table 12-8 *Median amounts received from different sources of income by London working-class elderly people, by age and gender*

	65-69	70-74	75-79	80+	65+	Total
1928-30 males						
State Benefits	10	10	10	10	10	731
Employment	55	40	(34)	(10)	50	285
Subletting	11	15	14	(21)	13	234
Family	(8)	(10)	(7)	(11)	10	32
Other	24	10	10	(9)	10	96
Overall	36	20	20	10	21	866
1979-81 males						
NI pension	25	25	24	24	24	346
SB	11	12	(10)	(15)	11	80
Employment	52	(31)	(23)	–	46	46
Occ. pensions	11	7	9	9	9	180
Savings	1	1	(1)	–	1	63
Overall	40	35	34	35	36	364
1928-30 females						
State Benefits	10	10	10	10	10	1038
Employment	18	15	(3)	(14)	15	138
Subletting	13	20	20	(13)	16	150
Family	8	10	(10)	(6)	8	76
Other	(9)	15	(10)	(8)	10	47
Overall	10	10	10	10	10	1232
1979-81 females						
NI pension	21	22	23	24	23	490
SB	12	11	10	13	12	189
Employment	39	(15)	(16)	–	30	30
Occ. pensions	5	4	3	(3)	4	73
Savings	1	1	(1)	(1)	1	66
Overall	25	28	29	31	28	505

Notes: 1) numbers in brackets indicate values based upon small numbers;
2) '-' indicates empty cells;
3) data for 1928-30 in shillings; data for 1979-81 have been deflated using the Retail Price Deflator to give 1980 values.

166

have slightly higher median incomes from state pensions than women, though the inequality largely disappears with increasing age. Neither London nor the working class experienced different median incomes from state pensions. Prior to the introduction of the state earnings related pension scheme (SERPS) therefore, the pension was not discriminatory between classes, and nor perhaps between regions. This is not true of income from SB, however, the levels of which undoubtedly reflect the higher housing costs associated with London. Region in this case has a large discriminatory effect, while class has none at all.

For many of those elderly people employed in 1928-30, earnings were the most important source of income. Even for women, a fifth of whom worked, median earned incomes were significantly higher than median incomes from state benefits. But the relative importance of earnings declined with age: the percentage in some form of employment fell, as did the amount received. It has been noted that a lower proportion of London's working-class elderly worked in 1979-81 compared with 1928-30, but for men aged 65-69 years who did, median incomes were double the state pension. That was not quite the order of difference seen in 1928-30 when median earned income for men were four or five times as great as those from pensions. However, it is clear that employment, where it occurs, constitutes the second most important source of income for the elderly. This was certainly true for the early 1930s, and remains so today. Furthermore, it is true for men and for women, despite the pervasive experience of lower wages for women at both times. Looked at another way, the presence of paid employment proves to be the most important factor marking out one elderly person from another. This has become even more the case over the last fifty years.

In 1928-30 those in receipt of income from subletting, from kin, and from charity and savings could expect amounts similar to, or even greater than, the prevailing levels of state pension. In 1979-81 however, income from renting out rooms would be a useful but hardly comparable amount. Income from 'other sources', including kin, was even less important, and savings and occupational pensions, while they have become increasingly common as sources of income, have not contributed to those who enjoy them an amount which, as was the case in 1928-30, approaches that obtained from the state pension.

167

Much more could be said about these income data: about the near consistent pattern of gender inequality for all these other sources (with the exception of subletting in 1928-30, and income from other sources in 1979-81), and the general, but slight, decline across age groups. Likewise, the 'London effect' is apparent in the case of income from occupational pensions, though it is scarcely strong enough to offset the lower incomes of the working class from this source. The general findings, however, are clear. In 1979-81 income from the state was by far the most important determinant of the total income of the elderly, for all groups: working class, non-working class, London and non-London. Incomes from employment were relatively high, but few elderly people had any paid work, and fewer now than fifty years ago. Whereas, as was observed earlier, more of the working-class elderly drew on occupational pensions and savings, the amounts they could expect by 1979-81 were much less as a proportion of the state pension than in 1928-30. An analysis of median income from savings indicates that very large numbers drew on savings but also that they drew very lightly. The significance of incomes from rent and from families (i.e. 'other' sources) has declined, with fewer elderly people receiving a comparatively smaller amount. In 1928-30 the family, in the very few cases where it helped elderly relatives financially, contributed a significant sum; by 1979-81 even this could not be argued. This may of course be precisely because of the greater access to state benefits and occupational pensions: in the 1930s it is clear that those in receipt of income from kin turn out to have been proportionately disadvantaged in their access to income from employment, and savings and private pensions, compared with other elderly people. The family was, and perhaps still is, seen as a last resort, an unwilling and reluctant benefactor.

The shift then becomes one largely from employment, subletting and kin to the state and savings - but savings in the form of occupational pensions. It is growing access to the latter which has done most to boost non-state income levels. Table 12-9 summarizes this, and the class and regional differences noted earlier. It is evident that income from kin is less important now than in the 1930s, and that even then it accounted for only 3 per cent of the total income of the elderly.

Table 12-9 *Composition of income of elderly people by period (percentages)*

	1928-30	1979-81 All	Working class	London	London's working class
Earnings	34	16	10	21	16
State benefits	42				
old age pension		59	70	51	62
SB		5	8	7	12
Subletting	14	*	*	*	*
Other	7				
occ. pension		14	8	14	8
saving		6	3	6	2
Family	3	1	0	1	0
Total (=100%)	2,098	13,611	8,244	1,688	945

Note: * indicates less than 1 per cent

Conclusion

It has been tempting for some politicians and policy makers to look nostalgically back to the past, seeing it as a time of greater familial responsibility, and to suggest that the state should and could have a secondary, interventionist, role in supporting the elderly. Increasingly there are echoes of the 'good old days' of self-help and individual responsibility and an insistence on the need to return to them. In the light of what we have found about London over the half century since 1930, and about Britain as a whole in 1979-81, it is not clear how valid such calls are. Examining the changing relative importance of the family and the state suggests evidence of a diminished role for the family but that even in the 1930s this role was minimal.

Concurrently, there has been a tendency towards increasing headship, and more elderly people now live alone. However, it is not true that a large proportion of the elderly lived with kin in the late 1920s nor that, were the shift in household composition since then to be reversed, it would be sufficiently different to warrant changes in current support structures. Of course, low levels of co-residence do not necessarily imply familial neglect. Informal care could, and can, be provided by extensive kin networks living outside but nearby the household. However, Gordon (1988) found that high levels of out-migration reduced the number of kin living in close proximity and it is not clear in any case that extensive networks could, or can, be relied upon as a 'natural resource' upon which the elderly can draw.

The family were not an important source of financial assistance to the elderly in the past either. Where assistance was received, it did not approach that from the state and from independent means. The overwhelming importance of state income is in fact clearly demonstrated. There appears to be no time in the recent past when the state has taken a subsidiary role in income provision for the elderly. Coverage of state support has undoubtedly increased over time, but this has not been at the 'expense' of the family. Changes in the composition of income that have occurred, have largely involved a substitution of employment income in the past by occupational pensions and savings in the present. The role of the family in financial support has always been a minor one.

This analysis then serves to reinforce the conclusions of earlier work which suggests that those who argue that the family should *once again* shoulder some of the increasing burden presented by an ageing population, need to rethink their assumptions about the capacity and desirability of the family to look after its elderly relatives. Furthermore, present demographic patterns mean that the elderly in future will have fewer descendent kin upon whom they might need to depend, will live in smaller households, and will experience a greater risk of familial and marital dissolution (Eversley, 1982). Women, who shoulder much of the burden of informal care (Evandrou, 1990), are now spending more years in employment, a trend which will continue in the face of a relatively diminishing working population. With long-run economic, demographic and social changes acting to make familial care more difficult, it is likely that, in the future, the family may be unwilling or unable to expand its role in the care of the elderly.

Acknowledgements

The authors wish to thank the Office of Population, Censuses and Surveys for permission to use the General Household Survey and the ESRC Data

Archive. Thanks are also due to the BLPES, London School of Economics, for use of their archives with regard to the NSOL. The archival sources used in this study are: (i) the Household Survey cards of the NSOL; 50 boxes; (ii) Folio 2\1, NSOL, Draft Chapter on 'The Aged Poor'. The research was supported by the ESRC (reference number G00 23 2344) and by the Welfare State Programme at the Suntory Toyota International Centre for Economics and Related Disciplines. We are grateful to Maria Evandrou, John Hills and Paul Johnson for their helpful comments on earlier drafts.

13 The meaning and experience of 'home' in later life

Andrew J. Sixsmith

The concept of 'home' is central to current health and welfare policy for the elderly. The Wagner Report (1988) emphasises the advantages of 'staying put' in a familiar environment or supportive neighbourhood. Reports by the Audit Commission (1986) and Griffiths (1988) have focused on how to provide effective community care in order to support people in their own homes.

However, the nature of the relationship between person and home in later life is little understood. Of the growing literature on the meaning of home (Altman and Warner, 1985; Sixsmith, 1986b), only a few studies have addressed the specific dimension of old age (Peace et al, 1983; Willcocks et al, 1987; Csikszentmihalyi and Rochberg-Halton, 1981). Without the insights provided by basic research, there is always a danger that inadequate or invalid concepts and principles may be translated into policy and welfare practice. For instance, in residential settings for the elderly, too much emphasis has been given to functional support, and too little to the general quality of life. Furthermore, policies for the elderly in the community have focused on instrumental issues, such as the development of financial schemes and domiciliary care that aim to provide the basic necessities that will keep elderly people independent for as long as possible. Although these are worthwhile objectives, they seem to be defined mainly by the professionals concerned. To reiterate a question put by Tinker (1977), do we 'really know what the elderly want or do we as a society provide what we think they want, or ought to want?'

Perhaps this results from a tendency to view ageing as a 'problem' (Goldberg, 1983). This is evident in the dominant concern with the minority of people who are living in specialist accommodation for the elderly. Even within community based studies, attention has focused mainly on the problems of planned accommodation and issues such as the segregation of the elderly (Butler, 1986). By focusing on housing in old age as a problem, research has limited our understanding of home as a normal part of living and has implicitly reinforced a negative image of old age. Few studies have examined the links that are commonly taken for granted between the older person and the home environment. There have been vague discussions of familiarity, attachment, and memories, but these have been without an adequate framework to synthesize all the disparate issues. Work by Rowles (1981), Howell (1983) and Golant (1984) have gone some way to filling this gap, but there is still a need for basic research. The objective of the present study is to provide a coherent and general account of home experience in later life.

Approach

The research must begin from the experiences of older people themselves, prior to the definition of 'problem' areas and the building of theories. Concern is not so much with the home environment as a physical entity or commodity, but with the home as a meaningful context for everyday life. This has conceptual and methodological implications. As Rapoport (1982, p. 144) argues, 'the environment that affects people is the perceived and cognizable environment ... and it must be approached phenomenologically'. To this end it is important to look at the older people as individuals who determine and interpret their own situations.

The exploration of the relationship with home is based on in-depth interviews with over sixty people, aged over 65, in Newcastle-upon-Tyne. In addition, follow up interviews were conducted and a core of six people participated as case studies. Participants were encouraged to expand on their views as much as possible and to talk freely about their own feelings and experiences. This generated considerable qualitative data. The basic approach to analysis was to reduce accounts to basic meaning categories through content analysis. Case studies were used to illustrate and develop the emergent themes. The responses of the older people were compared with two smaller groups of unemployed and employed people.

What is 'home'?

The starting point of the empirical investigation was the content analysis of participants' accounts of what 'home' meant to them. A complex

Table 13-1 *Meanings of home: elderly and comparison groups*

Category	Frequency of mention of categories of home (percentages).			
	All	Over 65	Unemployed	Employed
Family	56	40	82	82
Comfort	20	22	36	24
It's what you make it	19	18	18	24
Happiness	17	18	23	6
Like to return	16	20	14	6
Arrange place how I like	16	15	9	29
Possessions	17	5	18	53
Familiarity	15	16	9	18
Privacy	15	18	14	6
Do what you want	16	15	18	18
Ownership	13	16	9	6
Atmosphere	13	7	23	18
Security	13	15	18	0
Lived in	12	5	18	24
Physical aspects	12	11	5	24
Friendly people around	11	16	5	0
Memories	9	15	0	0
Good neighbours	7	15	0	0
Self	7	2	14	18
Things to do	5	9	0	0
Convenient locality	5	7	0	6
Belonging	4	4	0	12
Bring friends back	4	2	5	12
Proximity to family	1	0	9	0
Number (= 100%)	88	49	17	22

174

picture emerged. Although there were also considerable differences between them, there was a set of attributes that were mentioned by most people when asked to define what home meant. It was possible to identify consistent themes within their accounts and twenty-five meaning categories such as 'family', 'comfort', and 'privacy' were defined (Table 13-1). These broadly coincide with other studies of popular conceptualisations of home (Sixsmith, 1986b).

Interestingly, there were clear differences in the usage of certain meaning categories between the elderly and comparison groups (Table 13-2). Some meanings were common to all three groups: 'comfort', 'family', 'do what you want' and 'it's what you make it', for example. Other meanings were particularly common among the older group, such as 'memories' and 'good neighbours'. Some meanings were shared by them with either the employed or the unemployed group, perhaps indicating some common underlying characteristic. Other meanings, notably 'self' and 'possessions', were absent from the accounts of older participants.

Table 13-2 *Meanings of 'home': comparisons between elderly, unemployed and employed people*

Common to all three groups:	It's what you make it Comfort Family Do what you want
Just the elderly group:	Good neighbours Memories Friendly people around Ownership
The elderly and unemployed groups:	Happiness Like to return Privacy Security
The elderly and employed groups:	Familiarity Arrange place how I like Physical aspects
The unemployed and employed but not the elderly group:	Lived in Atmosphere Possessions Self

What is indicated is a value that is consciously placed on certain aspects of home experience, which may be predicated by a feeling of loss or change in circumstances in later life. For example, home as a place for happiness is something that is appreciated by unemployed and elderly participants. Several older people said that when they were young their home was just a place for coming and going and living in. It is often not until later that a person realises the happiness of family life and how much this is a part of their home experience. The analysis points to a number of concerns that underlie the particular meanings that older people associate with home.

Firstly, older people, through personal choice and by force of circumstance, seem to be more oriented towards their homes than are younger people. For instance, the emphasis on home as a 'refuge' appears signficant for older people. The home may become increasingly important as other social roles are superceded.

Secondly, older people appear to be more concerned with instrumental aspects of home than the younger people interviewed. This may be related to a desire to remain at home and maintain an independent life. If an increasingly frail older person is to stay at home, then the environment in which s/he lives must afford support. Access to local amenities may be important, and the informal support offered by neighbours can be invaluable.

A third theme is that older people may have a deeper personal concern for their homes. The issue of 'memories' is of particular significance, past associations affecting the present experience of home. This aspect is notably absent from the accounts of younger participants.

Thus these three themes, home focus, independence and attachment, are central to the understanding of home experience in later life and are now explored in turn.

Home focus

Home focus refers to a general tendency for home to take on a greater significance in later life. A common image of the lives of 'the elderly' is that of an inexorable spatial constriction, with a concomitant increase in the significance of the home environment. Although simplistic, the participants' use of places supports this general image. In comparison with younger groups, the older group had a more restricted geographical range, had a smaller repertoire of places and spent less time outside the house. The great majority (80%) of the older participants themselves agreed that home does become more important in later life. They suggested a number of possible reasons for this.

- The interests and activities of some older people become centred on the home.

- Many older people simply spend more time at home, due to fewer non-home places that cater for elderly people; lack of money; increasing physical frailty; a positive preference for the home as opposed to other places.

- One's home is perceived to be something that is solid, which affords a sense of permanence and security in later life.

- Home is also a place of refuge and privacy. The seclusion of the home was preferred by a number of the elderly participants.

- As older people face the reality or possibility of increasing frailty, the home is seen as a source of independence and personal control.

- Many older people felt that they had grown more attached to their homes in later life.

In some ways, 'home focus' can be seen as a form of 'spatial disengagement' in that a decreasing social life space is paralleled by a decreasing spatial range. Participants' accounts of their lives showed that they had had to reorientate their lives in some way. Often this is a response to traumatic life events, while for others later life is characterised by a gradual reorientation. In the present context, the interesting issue is that changes in one's life in general and changes in one's environmental experience go hand in hand. This is not just a matter of environmental constraint. The home can be used as a resource for coping with later life. The home can be a basis for new interests and activities and can be a source of emotional support. In this sense, the home presents opportunities for developing one's life in a positive way and certainly the preference for the home environment was very prevalent amongst participants.

177

The case of Mrs. Charlton is interesting in this respect. Although Mrs. Charlton is a very friendly and chatty person, she prefers to lead a quiet life at home:

> I went out last night to Whickham View bingo. I never go usually, but I went last night. It was great and I really enjoyed myself. I met people I used to work with and I got to hear all the news. I really enjoyed it. I didn't like the bingo particularly, but I liked seeing my friends. I won't go again particularly - I wouldn't go regular. I am a home bird. I was there and I was thinking 'there is a programme on telly I'm missing', and I was disappointed that I had missed it. That's how much I go out at night!

For Mrs. Charlton, focus on the home is a matter of personal choice. She has plenty of opportunities for visiting or doing things outside the home. Yet she chooses a more solitary existence. She sees herself very much as a 'loner', a characteristic that is reflected in her geographical experience. The home can play a major part in maintaining the life of the 'loner'. The basic affordance of the home is that it is the domain of the individual, where the external world of others can be effectively excluded. For Mrs. Charlton, home is a refuge, a place of sanctuary to which she can return:

> I like to be in my own home best. The world is changing. You enjoy seeing the changes, but it is a sin to see a lot of the lovely old places being knocked down and that. I love to go out and see all the changes, but I like to come back and get home. I'll tell you what it is like. I went to Denmark once and I was seasick on the boat. I was glad to be back on terra firma. That is what it is like to be back home. I think 'thank God I am home'. It's the only place you can feel like that. I like to go out, but there is nothing I like better than getting back.

In the case of Mrs. Charlton it is possible to see the congruence of psychic and physical space. Mrs. Charlton is essentially introspective, a focus that is reflected in, and perhaps reinforced by, a spatial focus on the home.

It is also important to place home experience within the wider biographical experience of the individual. Mrs. Charlton had been widowed for six years. She responded to the solitude of home as a place of quietness and of calm, rather than as a place of emptiness and desolation. As mentioned earlier, she sees her home as 'terra firma' as opposed to the 'sea' of the outside world. This is a powerful image; the tranquility afforded by the home is clearly very important to Mrs. Charlton. It also

178

indicates the nature of her readjustment to life alone. The losses in her life are regretted, but her statements imply that her situation is construed positively. There is a sense of relief, that she can now lead a quiet home life in her later years.

Independence

'Independence' was a recurrent theme in participants' accounts of their home experience. Although used freely by the elderly themselves, academics and welfare professionals, the term is not well understood. A conceptual analysis (Sixsmith, 1986a) showed that independence is a complex term that has a number of meanings: not being physically dependent; self-direction or control; and the absence of feelings of obligation (Table 13-3). In natural discourse, the specific meaning depends on the context in which it is being used. For example, when participants talked about old people's homes, the main concern was with loss of 'self-direction'. People in old people's homes are perceived as not being able to do as they please or as not in control of their own destiny. In contrast, talking about the prospect of living with relatives involved the loss of independence in terms of 'obligation'. People do not want to be a 'burden' to their family.

Independence is an important value amongst older people. But why is this? How does it become so? Is it perceived differently in later life?

Table 13-3   *Structure of the home-independence relationship*

Mode of independence	Self/others orientation	Role of home
Not dependent	Self Others	Do things for yourself Not depending on anybody
Self-direction	Self Others	Can do what you want Nobody tells you what to do
Obligation	Self Others	Symbolic of independence Not beholden to anybody

One can suggest that in the face of its loss, independence can no longer be taken for granted, as in earlier years. The possibility of persons losing their independence, however they define it, demonstrates clearly to them just how important a sense of independence is to them.

Although home and independence are components of our everyday lives, they are given significance in individual terms only because they are contextualized within our whole life experience. In particular, our desires, objectives and expectations of the future construct a changing set of cognitions within which we orientate our day to day experiences. Thus, the ways in which a place facilitates or obstructs our aims has direct implications for the experience of that place as home. Being independent is not just a matter of feeling independent, as there must be some basis of independence in actuality. Although independence is a highly symbolic and subjective experience, the home provides a necessary material context for being independent, which is itself an essential component of home experience in later life. The home is not simply a house, but a meaningful context for human action. The home affords independence in all its modes, by providing a physical boundary between the individual and others, and by defining a space that is uniquely the domain of the individual.

The significance of home also depends on the ageing individual. Many older participants in the research were aware of the possibility of losing their independence, and the desire to remain independent may be a prime consideration, bringing into the foreground the role of the home. The home becomes the place where independence can be best preserved, and as such becomes a focus of concern. As independence becomes personally more significant, so does the value that an older person places on their home as a material basis of independence.

The evaluation by participants of different types of living arrangements for the elderly illustrates this point. For example, attitudes towards old people's homes were generally negative. A move to a home is not just a loss of physical independence, but is also seen as a loss of control and self. For those people who had some form of disability, the prospect could amount to 'dread'. In an illuminating study of older people faced with the prospect of moving from apartments to a nursing home, Morgan (1983) described the coping strategies that people use and the lengths they will go to avoid this move. For example, people would try to hide physical problems from medical authorities. The relative independence offered by an apartment was invariably worth physical suffering and the possibility of premature death. A shorter but more fulfilling life was preferred to the 'social death' (Kalish, 1966) implied by admission to the nursing home.

It is argued here that one of the central transactions between a person and his or her home is 'independence'. Independence is a function of both the individual's perceptions and the material constraints and opportunities of a place. It has already been stressed that despite the subjective and symbolic nature of independence, it would be wrong to simply talk in ideal terms. How a person perceives and values independence is structured by the material world.

From this perspective, it is possible to understand the growing significance of the home in terms of the transaction 'independence', which links together the ageing person's awareness of the life changes that are common in later years, and the home as a means of negotiating these changes. The home is a flexible thing in how it is used, but is a constant factor symbolically. The home remains a link with the past in suggesting that one is still able to do the things that one has always done. The home also allows one to maintain control over oneself, to remain 'true' to oneself. Finally, the home is symbolic of the values that one has always had. Ultimately, it is these symbolic qualities that are of greatest significance to the individual.

It is possible to link independence to the notion of identity. At one level the body signifies absolute individuality, while at other levels the individual becomes subsumed within group identities, such as race or nation. This is not to say that the concept of independence is equivalent to concepts of identity or self. To construe independence as an abstract phenomenon would be wrong, as its behavioural aspects, such as 'being able to do what you want', are important components of how people understand independence. Independence is something that is directly experienced and is grounded in the material world. In experiential terms, independence is a more fundamental everyday concept that locates identity as 'identity in the world', or 'being in the world' (Heidegger, 1962; Starr, 1983).

The home plays an important part in framing the experience of independence and 'identity in the world', through the affordance of control. The home is a symbol of the individual, both as an expression of identity to others, and as a personal confirmation of the 'I' as distinct from 'others'. In a social context, old age is seen as a time of deterioration, loss of status and increased dependency. Symbolically, a person's home represents a denial of this, given the legitimate control that a person retains within the home domain.

Attachment to home

With the exception of Rowles (1978, 1981, 1983), surprisingly little attention has been given to emotional aspects of the relationship between ageing and the environment. Attachment is assumed to play an important part in the desire of most older people to 'stay put'. The present study likewise found that most of the participants had no desire to leave their present homes and had never even considered a move. A number of reasons were given for why they wished to stay where they were (Table 13-4). These included dislike of upheaval; fear of the unknown; preference for the present home; lack of suitable alternatives; lack of reasons for moving; and a feeling that the present home was their final home. Although the relationship between person and home is complex and individualistic, the research supports the common assumption that older people tend to be attached to their homes. This attachment has a number of dimensions including memories, familiarity, rootedness, and an awareness of the end of life.

Memories and home

One should not think of the act of remembering as being peculiar to older people. Memories are important for people throughout their lives. Yet the emphasis that is placed by most older people on remembering the past indicates a special role for memories in later life. The exploration of the nature and the role of memories in the home experience of older people must begin from an understanding of the nature of remembering in general in everyday life (Sixsmith, 1988).

Two modes of remembering need to be considered. Firstly, reminiscence can be defined as the conscious recall of the past. Reminiscence, the focus of a good deal of gerontological theory (Butler, 1963; Erikson, 1968; Coleman, 1986), is usually seen as a way of coming to

Table 13-4 *Why older people stay put: the responses of 36 participants*

Category	Observation	Number of mentions
Memories, contentment	Reminisce, dreamworld	2
	Fond memories	3
	Happy and settled	5
	Contented	3
Rooted	Lived there that long	8
	Attached	4
	Used to it, settled	8
	Feels right	2
	Your habitat	2
	Rooted	4
	It's part of you and your life	2
The individual	Depends on person	2
	Can't imagine why people feel like this	1
End of life	Too old, no time to settle down	1
	You hope you can enjoy it while you can	1
	Come to end of life	1
	Stay here till we die	2
	Ready for box if you move	1
Benefits of staying put	You know people around you	1
	No point in leaving	4
	Have it exactly how I like	1
	Have their knick knacks around them	1
	It's your ambition, achievement	1
Problems of leaving	Have to leave friends	1
	Might not get on with new neighbours	1
	Couldn't get a good alternative	4
	Have to make new friends	2
	You couldn't get used to it	2
	Upheaval	5
	Couldn't share with anyone else	1
	Nowhere else to go	1
	Have to start all over again	1

183

terms with the experience of growing old. The notion that remembering is a coping process, however, fails to capture the full significance of memories for older people. Many memories occur spontaneously (Salaman, 1970) and, unlike conscious efforts to recollect the past, these memories come unbidden. They are often accompanied by the emotions of direct experience and a sense of reliving the past. The home environment may play an important part in the process of remembering, whatever its precise nature. This relationship has a number of facets:

Memories of the home. Memories of events imply memories of places. The home is a scene of family life and consequently constitutes much of the substance of a person's memories. These memories are pertinent to people of all ages. However, they perhaps take on a greater significance in the context of old age. The loss of a husband or wife, or the moving away of children, may prompt a re-evaluation of past events, and memories of home may be accorded greater significance as a consequence. This is evident in the accounts presented in this chapter.

Memories by the home. The house, its rooms, and objects in the home provide cues which evoke memories. The associations between the physical environment and the past can be very strong, to the extent that some older people feel the presence of a deceased spouse when they are in the house. Sixsmith (1988) provides an interesting case study of this phenomenon and suggests that the concept of spontaneous remembering is relevant. Memories for a few moments can vividly recreate past episodes in the present. People are not simply restricted to the here and now. The faculties of imagination and remembering can expand the experiential world far beyond the confines of the present. This may be important for housebound people or for those who live alone and whose lives may seem superficially empty. Rowles (1978) suggests that fantasy and remembering can make you free.

Home as the place for memories. The home is perceived to have a special role in preserving memories, or as the place in which reminiscence takes place. The role of home cannot be dissociated from the significance placed upon memories of the past. For people who have suffered loss or significant change, the desire to keep the past alive is paralleled by a desire to maintain the home as the scene of past events. Hence, many people expressed the feeling that to leave their homes would be to leave the past behind; something which they are reluctant to do. The home is seen as a way of preserving memories, and preserving the continuity of a valued past.

Familiarity with the home environment

For many people their home and neighbourhood are places that they have known for a long time. To leave such a familiar place may involve leaving behind family and friends as well as a valued locale and house. Conversely, people are often apprehensive about having to move to an unfamiliar place. This attitude perhaps reflects a need for security, stability and order, one which is fulfilled by one's home. This need for security implies a conservative impulse within place experience. There are other contrasting impulses, such as the desire for adventure and novelty which may represent a need to move on. However, within the present study, older participants emphasised their desire to stay put and were often apprehensive of moving to a new place. Place familiarity in later life has two dimensions: security and temporal experience. Regarding security, increasing frailty and deteriorating faculties may make everyday life a stressful process. Some participants felt secure in their homes because they knew their houses intimately. Acting in and on the dwelling over time had provided them with a habitual memory of the place that can be both psychologically and instrumentally supportive. Without this knowledge of the familiar environment, people may feel vulnerable. Familiarity is particularly significant for those who are less physically competent. In one case, an intimate knowledge of room layouts and floor surfaces was an essential part of remaining instrumentally independent.

A second theme defines familiarity in terms of temporal experience. Being at home does not just comprise perceptions of the present, but also memories of the place. These relict impressions may outweigh the reality of the present. For instance, memories of a happy family life may still contribute to a happy home atmosphere even when a person lives alone. The physical environment fosters a feeling of familiarity, in spite of considerable social change. In a sense, familiarity can be illusory. For example, a number of participants said that they knew everybody in their neighbourhood, despite the loss of most of their social contacts. Older people may find it difficult to reconcile potent images of the past with changed present circumstances.

Rootedness

People interpret their situations. In trying to resolve the often contradictory strands of their place experiences, they use terms such as 'familiar' to describe extremely complex situations. These terms are not simply descriptive, but in turn define the experience of place. Familiarity has a particular logic: to live in a place for a long time is seen to afford familiarity and implies entailments of knowledge, intimacy and being at ease. This interpretation may even run counter to actual circumstances, such as continual change in the neighbourhood. The outcome of using the term 'familiar' is to be familiar, and emphasises the role of language and imagery in defining reality for an individual.

Familiarity with home found its most common expression when participants talked about having roots in a place. Rootedness is a metaphor which likens human existence to that of plants. For example:

> Of course your home becomes more important when you are older. That's where your roots are. I have seen two or three people who have moved and they weren't long gone till one of them died. It depends on their circumstances. They might brood and not settle down; like shifting plants in the garden.

The analogy between people and plants is powerfully expressed by this participant. The way in which participants used the term involved a number of dimensions.

- Being rooted is linked to length of residence. People are said to 'put down roots', which over time are seen to become almost permanent.

- The place where one has roots nourishes and sustains the individual and is therefore fundamental to existence.

- The relationship between person and home requires careful 'cultivation' and care if the individual is to flourish.

- The necessity of having roots implies that to be rootless is unnatural.

- To move from one's home is to be 'uprooted'. This is to be in a precarious situation, as the person will eventually wither and die if they cannot put down roots elsewhere.

- Being uprooted implies being removed by force with no control over the situation.

The metaphor of roots is powerful and goes further than mere expression. Such imagery is part of the reality for the individual and has implications for how they act in the world (Lakoff and Johnson, 1980). For example, some people felt that they were too old to move and to have time to put roots down elsewhere. Some felt that if old people are uprooted they will invariably deteriorate and die. These are powerful images that contribute to a strong desire to stay put.

Home and the end of life

A number of authors (Cottle and Klinberg, 1974; Ward, 1979; Lieberman and Tobin, 1983) suggest that a sense of impending death is a central feature of the psychology of old age. This awareness is part of the practical consciousness, the tacit knowledge, that is applied to the way actions are conducted. In particular, the formulation and carrying through of longer term plans may be perceived to be futile. The basic limitation of time on the capacity to undertake a longer term action may be a significant practical consideration. Participants' feelings about the future are summarised in Table 13-5.

Many of the participants suggested that death could occur at any time and that there was little point in undertaking new projects. For some the major objective in life was to maintain the present situation; to live as long as possible and to avoid becoming dependent. For others, the main concern for the future lay with children. Participants saw the future as being limited, and most were simply concerned with making the 'best of things'. Participants did have objectives and hopes, but these were primarily a matter of extending their present situations for as long as possible; to go on 'living life as I am doing now', to maintain good health and to avoid dependence.

Table 13-5 *Hopes and plans for the future*

Category	Observation	Number of mentions
Maintaining the present	Carry on the way I have done	5
	Go on living as healthily as possible	2
	Keep going until last moment	4
	Take life as it comes	1
	Keep things as they are	2
	Live as long as I can	4
	Just enjoy ourselves	2
	Make best of things	2
	Lads keep coming to see me	1
No prospects	What future?	8
	No prospects	9
	What plans can you have at this age?	4
	Just the daily routine	1
	Reminisce (nothing to look forward to)	1
Fear of dependency	Go peacefully	1
	To live in my own house	2
	Not to go into old folks home	2
	As long as I can get about	2
	Couldn't cope with change	1
	Worried about the way it will end	1
	Hate to be dependent	1
Specific objectives	Move to where friends live	1
	Like to go abroad	1
	Take up evening classes	1
	Like my knees put right	2
	Win pools	1
Negative	Lonely	1
	Cannot get out	1
	No money	1
	Can't hurry up	1
	Scared to leave home	2
	Had a bad deal	1
Concern	Hope children are O.K.	8
	Hope for country, world	2

The relationship between the older person and home should be seen in this wider life context. The process of finding and moving to a new home is a process that can extend over a considerable time. But perhaps more significant than the time it takes, is the radical revision of one's life that follows. In a new home one has to establish new patterns of living, new contacts, and to get used to new places and people. This represents the kind of upheaval in both material and symbolic terms that was often abhorrent to participants. The result is a preference for the familiarity of the home, a place that is intimate, that affords a sense of stability and security. This was often expressed as being a 'final refuge':

> Well, it's that people have come to the end of their life and don't want to start a new one. When you get to that stage, you just sort of think that there is no point in moving.

> The trouble with moving is being sure of getting a good place and making friends in a new place. The trouble is though, that you haven't the time to make real friends properly or settle down if you are already old.

Theoretical considerations

This chapter has been aimed at providing some insights into the relationship between person and home in later life. It has also been possible to point to three themes that underlie the experiential domains of home focus, independence and attachment.

Temporality of home experience

The first theme focuses on the temporality of home experience. Home is not something that is 'in' the environment, nor is it some kind of idealistic notion on the part of the dweller. Throughout the discussion, the emphasis has been on the home as a transaction between person and place. This perspective requires an investigation into both how the individual's wider lifeworld impinges upon the experience of home, and how home experience in turn bears upon this wider experience. The characteristic picture that emerged from the research involves both continuity and change. Most of the people interviewed had lived in their homes for many years and the home was a medium for continuity in their lives, for example through memories. Conversely, most had had to come to terms with actual and potential changes in their later lives: crises, dependence, and the imminence of death. In reorienting their lives in the face of these circumstances, they reorientate their home experience, both behaviourally and cognitively. Thus the temporality that characterizes ageing and home experience can be summarised as follows.

- *The past.* Individuals have a sense of having a history. The past, in terms of personal experiences, has implications for their home experience through its memories and familiarity.

- *The present.* Individuals have to cope with the life changes that characterize later life. The home represents an important resource for coping and many older people believe that the home takes on a greater personal significance.

- *The future.* The awareness of death or the possibility of physical dependency lends considerable symbolic value to the home. For many older people, the home is a means of preserving independence, individuality and identity in the face of a threatening future.

Coming into consciousness

A second theme relates to the coming into consciousness of the personal significance of home. One could suggest that in many ways the relationship between person and place is the same for both younger people and for older people. For example, the 'memories' category was uniquely associated with elderly respondents. Does this mean that younger people have no memories associated with their home? Of course not, it is rather a matter of becoming aware of, and expressing, the significance of memories in relation to the home, a tendency which was characteristic of the older participants. As one person put it 'you only realise how important your home is when you are older'. The inference from this is that home experience is a duality. On the one hand, there are those aspects of which we are heedful and others which are habitual or immediately forgotten. Natsoulas (1983) provides insight into why this occurs by referring to the distinction between being aware and being

190

conscious of being aware. Although this reflexivity is characteristic of human consciousness, it is not pervasive:

> ... awarenesses of the environment do occur when habitual behaviours are produced, but there is less utility in becoming conscious of such awarenesses, as compared to the awarenesses involved when we are uncertain concerning how to respond. (Natsoulas, 1983, p. 37).

The 'coming into consciousness' of home is related to the first theme of experiential temporality. Old age is characterized by actual or potential life changes in life circumstances and the awareness of finitude. It is in the context of these changes that a person becomes aware of his or her situation and the need to respond. This in turn makes conspicuous the role of home within one's life and its potential value in responding to change.

Role of language in framing environmental experience

A third theme is the role of language in framing environmental experience. How people describe their homes and neighbourhoods is not something that can be taken at face value. The present research mainly consisted of a systematic analysis of participants' discourse, where the aim was to explicate as precisely as possible the meanings that underlie the commonsense notions of 'home'. As the research progressed, it became evident that the way people talked about their homes was not simply descriptive, but also constitutive, of their environmental experience. For instance, the use of metaphors such a 'roots' involved a view of person and place interaction that served to define the possibilities for future actions.

The idea that language structures the way we think about the world and act in it, is examined by Wittgenstein (1958). He argues that language should not be seen as directly representative of an absolute reality, but as a 'tool'. People actively use language to shape their lives and to achieve some objective. Indeed, Wittgenstein uses the term 'language game' as a metaphor for communication. As a game, language is primarily a social activity which is governed by rules. One should look at the rules of the game; the way in which words are used in the context of a particular situation.

The significance of this is illustrated by the way people use the term 'independence'. Understanding it requires an appreciation of the role it plays within older people's lives. From this perspective, it is possible to link the role of the home to the key concept of the life review in old age. The life review can be seen as a 'coming into consciousness' of personally valued events in the past, at the time of becoming aware of impending death. But more than that, it is an interpretation or evaluation of one's life situation as a whole. It is in this context, that the use of language generates an understanding of home as a focus of concern that relates to ideas about independence, attachment and life.

Bibliography

Age Concern (1989), *A Buyer's Guide to Sheltered Housing*, 3rd edition, Mitcham: Age Concern.

Age Concern (1990), *Information Circular*, April, p. 1.

Allan, J.D. and Hall, B.A. (1988), 'Challenging the focus of technology - a critique of the medical model in a changing health care system', *Advances in Nursing Science*, 10.3, pp. 22-34.

Altman, I. and Werner C. (1985), *Home Environments: Human Behaviour and the Environment*, New York: Plenum.

Anderson, M. (1971), *Family Structure in Nineteenth Century Lancashire*, Cambridge: Cambridge University Press.

Andrews, J., Fairley, A. and Hyland, M. (1970), 'A geriatric day ward in an English hospital', *Journal of the American Geriatrics Society*, 18.5, pp. 378-386.

Armstrong, W.A. (1972), 'A note on the household structure of mid nineteenth century York in comparative perspective', in *Household and Family in Past Time*, (Eds. P. Laslett and R. Wall), Cambridge: Cambridge University Press.

Association of Directors of Social Services (1981), *Staffing and Dependency in Homes for the Elderly*, Northern Branch, Carlisle.

Atchley, R.C. (1976), *The Sociology of Retirement*, Cambridge, Massachusetts: Schenkman.

Audit Commission (1986), *Making a Reality of Community Care*, London: HMSO.

Beauchesne, M.N. (1985), *Retirement: a Time of Transition: Belgium*, Dublin: European Foundation for Living and Working Conditions.

Bebbington, A., Davies, B.P. and Associates (1989), *Resources, Needs and Outcomes in Community-Based Care*, Aldershot: Gower Press.

Beck, S.H. (1983), 'Adjustment to, and satisfaction with, retirement', *Journal of Gerontology*, 37.5, pp. 616-624.

Bennett, A. (1988), 'A cream cracker under the settee', *Talking Heads*, London: BBC Publications.

Beresford, P. and Croft, S. (1986), *Whose Welfare?*, Brighton: Lewis Cohen Urban Studies Centre.

Bonny, S. (1984), 'Who cares in Southwark', Rochester: Association of Carers.

Booth, C. (ed.) (1892-97), *Life and Labour of the People of London*, 9 volumes, London: Macmillan.

Bornat, J. (1985), 'Reminiscence: the state of the art', *New Age*, 31, pp. 14-15.

Bowl, R., Taylor, H., Taylor, M. and Thomas, N. (1978), 'Day care for the elderly in Birmingham', Mimeograph for the Social Services Unit, University of Birmingham.

Bradshaw, J.R. and Gibbs, I. (1988), *Public Support for Private Residential Care*, Aldershot: Gower Press.

British Association of Social Workers (1984), 'Practice notes for social workers and registration officers working with the private and voluntary residential sector'.

Brocklehurst, J.C. (1964), 'The work of a geriatric day hospital', *Gerontologia Clinica*, 6.3, pp. 151-166.

Brocklehurst, J.C. and Tucker J.S. (1980), 'Progress in geriatric day care', London: King Edward's Hospital Fund for London.

Bulmer, M. (1987), *The Social Basis of Community Care*, London: Croom Helm.

Butler, A. (1986), 'Housing and the elderly in Europe', *Social Policy and Administration*, 20.2, pp. 136-152.

Butler, R.N. (1963), 'The life review: an interpretation of reminiscence in the aged', *Psychiatry*, 26, pp. 65-76.

Bytheway, B. and Johnson, J. (1990), 'On defining ageism', *Critical Social Policy*, 29.

Cahn, E. (1986), 'Service credits: a new currency for the welfare state', STICERD Welfare State Programme Discussion Paper, London School of Economics.

Cantley, C. and Smith, G. (1987), 'Day care for the elderly', in *Why Day Care?*, Research Highlights in Social Work 14, (Ed. G.W. Horobin), London: Jessica Kingsley Publishers.

Carter, J. (1981), *Day Services for Adults - Somewhere to Go*, London: George Allen and Unwin.

Central Council for Education and Training in Social Work, (1989), 'Requirements and regulations for the Diploma in Social Work', Paper 30.

Challis, L., Fuller, S., Henwood, M., Klein, R., Plowden, B., Webb, A., Whittingham, P. and Wistow, G. (1988), *Joint Approaches to Social Policy: Rationality and Practice*, Cambridge: Cambridge University Press.

Charmaz, K. (1983), 'Loss of self - a fundamental form of suffering in the chronically ill', *Sociology of Health and Illness*, 5.2, pp. 168-195.

Clegg, P.E. (1978), 'Day care for the elderly in the Metropolitan Borough of Kirklees', University of Bradford Social Work Unit.

Coid, J. and Crome, P. (1986), 'Bed blocking in Bromley', *British Medical Journal*, 292, pp. 1253-1256.

Coleman, A. (1982), *Preparation for Retirement in England and Wales*, Leicester: National Institute for Adult Education.

Coleman, P.G. (1986), *Ageing and Reminiscence Processes*, Chichester: John Wiley.

Coles, O.B. (1985), 'The dependency of old people in residential care: interpreting the trends', *Social Services Research*, 5.

Coles, O.B. (1990), 'Residential options for elderly mentally infirm people: main research report', Durham Social Services Department.

Cooper, J. (1980), 'Groupwork with elderly people in hospital', Keele: Beth Johnson Foundation.

Cosin, L. (1954), 'The place of the day hospital in the geriatric unit', *Practitioner*, 172(1031), pp. 552-559.

Cottle, T.J. and Klineberg S.L. (1974), *The Present of Things Future*, New York: Free Press.

Council of Europe (1977), *Preparation for Retirement*, Strasbourg.

Craig, H.M. and Edwards, J.E. (1983), 'Adaptation in chronic illness - an model for nurses', *Journal of Advanced Nursing*, 8, pp. 397-404.

Cribier, F. (1980), 'Changing retirement patterns: the experience of a cohort of Parisian salaried workers', *Ageing and Society*, 1.1, pp. 51-71.

Csikszentmihalyi, M. and Rochberg-Halton, E. (1981), *The Meaning of Things: Domestic Symbols and the Self*, Cambridge: Cambridge University Press.

Cumming, E. and Henry, W.E. (1961), *Growing Old: the Process of Disengagement*, New York: Basic Books.

Davies, B.P. (1986), 'American experiments to substitute homes for institutional longterm care: policy logic and evaluation', in *Dependency and Interdependency in Old Age: Theoretical Perspectives and Policy Alternatives*, (Eds. C. Phillipson, M. Bernard and P. Strang), London: Croom Helm.

Davies, B.P. (1988), 'Financing longterm social care: challenges for the Nineties', *Social Policy and Administration*, 22.2, pp. 97-114.

Davies, B.P. and Challis, D.J. (1986), *Matching Resources to Needs in Community Care*, Aldershot: Gower Press, for the PSSRU.

Davies, B.P. and Goddard, M. (1987a), 'The brokerage-only BRITSMO concept', PSSRU Discussion Paper, DP554.

Davies, B.P. and Goddard, M. (1987b), 'The insurability of the risk of long-term care', PSSRU Discussion Paper, DP556.

Davies, B.P. and Knapp, M.R.J. (1988), 'Costs and residential social care', in *Residential Care: the Research Reviewed*, Volume 2 of the Independent Review of Residential Care, (Ed. I. Sinclair, Chair: Lady G. Wagner), pp. 293-378.

Department of Health and Social Security (1971), *Hospital Geriatric Services*, London: HMSO.

Department of Health and Social Security (1981), *Growing Older*, Cmnd 8173, London: HMSO.

Department of Health and Social Security (1984), *Population, Pension Costs and Pensioners' Incomes*, London: HMSO.

Department of Health and Social Security (1985), *Reform of Social Security*, London: HMSO.

Department of Health (1989a), *Working for Patients*, London: HMSO.

Department of Health (1989b), *Caring for People: Care in the Next Decade and Beyond*, Cmnd 849, London: HMSO.

Dex, S. and Phillipson, C. (1986), 'Social policy and the older worker', in *Ageing and Social Policy*, (Eds. C. Phillipson and A. Walker), Aldershot: Gower Press.

de Wijs, R. (1981-2), '"PiZ" - Retirement in prospect', *Adult Education and Retirement*, European Bureau of Adult Education Newsletter, pp. 20-21.

Donnelly, A. (1986), 'Feminist social work with a women's group', *Social Work Monographs*, Norwich: University of East Anglia/BASW.

Droller, H. (1958), 'A geriatric outpatient department', *The Lancet*, 2(7049), pp. 739-741.

Eastman, M. (1976), 'Whatever happened to casework with the elderly?', *Age Concern Today*, 18, pp. 9-12.

Eichenbaum, L. and Orbach, S. (1982), *Outside In ... Inside Out Women's Psychology a Feminist Psychoanalytic Approach*, London: Penguin.

Erikson, E.H. (1968), *Identity: Youth and Crisis*, New York: Norton.

Estes, C.L. (1979), *The Aging Enterprise: a Critical Examination of Social Policies and Services for the Aged*, San Francisco: Jossey Bass.

Evandrou, M., Arber, S., Dale, A. and Gilbert, G.N. (1986), 'Who cares for the elderly? Family care provision and receipt of statutory service', in *Dependency and Interdependency in Old Age: Theoretical Perspectives and Policy Alternatives*, (Eds. C. Phillipson, M. Bernard and P. Strang), London: Croom Helm.

Evandrou, M. (1990), 'Mapping informal care nationally: challenging the invisibility ascribed to carers', STICERD Welfare State Programme Discussion Paper No. 20, London School of Economics.

Evans, G., Hughes, B. and Wilkin, D. (1981), *The Management of Mental and Physical Impairment in Non-Specialist Residential Homes for the Elderly*, Research Report No 4, Psychogeriatric Unit, University Hospital of South Manchester.

Evans, J.G. (1983), 'Integration of geriatric with general medical services in Newcastle', *Lancet*, 1, p. 1430.

Evers, H. (1985), 'The frail elderly women: emergent questions in ageing and women's health', in *Women, Health and Healing*, (Eds. E. Lewin and V. Olsen), London: Tavistock.

197

Eversley, D. (1982), 'The demography of retirement - prospects to the year 2000', in *Retirement Policy: the Next Fifty Years*, (Ed. M. Fogarty), London: Heinemann.

Falkingham, J. and Gordon, C. (1988), 'Fifty years on: the income and household composition of the elderly in Britain', STICERD Welfare State Programme Discussion Paper No. 35, London School of Economics.

Farndale, J. (1961), *The Day Hospital Movement in Great Britain*, Oxford: Pergamon Press.

Fennell, G., Emerson, A.R., Sidell, M. and Hague, A. (1981), 'Day centres for the elderly in East Anglia', Norwich: University of East Anglia.

Fiegehen, G. (1986), 'Income after retirement', *Social Trends*, 16, London: HMSO.

Finch, J. (1987), 'Family obligation and the life course', in *Rethinking the Life Cycle*, (Eds. A. Bryman, B. Bytheway, P. Allatt and T. Keil), Basingstoke: Macmillan Press.

Finch, J. and Groves, D. (1983), *A Labour of Love: Women, Work and Caring*, London: Routledge and Kegan Paul.

Finch, J. and Groves, D. (1985), 'Old girl, old boy: gender divisions in social work with the elderly', in *Women, the Family and Social Work*, (Eds. E. Brooks and A. Davis), London: Tavistock.

Firth, J. (1987), *Public Support for Residential Care*, Report of a Joint Central and Local Government Working Party, London: Department of Health and Social Security.

Ford, G. and Taylor, R. (1985), 'The elderly as underconsulters: a critical reappraisal', *Journal of the Royal College of General Practitioners*, 35, p.244-47.

Friedmann, E.A. and Havighurst, R.J. (1954), *The Meaning of Work and Retirement*, Chicago: University of Chicago Press.

Froggatt, A. (1985), 'Listening to the voices of older women, creativity and social work responses', in *Ageing: Recent Advances and Creative Responses*, (Ed. A. Butler), London: Croom Helm.

Fulgraff, B. (1986), 'Preparation for post-professional life: the state of the art in the Federal Republic of Germany', *Journal of Educational Gerontology*, 1.1, pp. 31-41.

General Records Office (1952), *Census of England and Wales 1951*, London: HMSO.

Glendenning, F. (1986), Editorial, *Journal of Educational Gerontology,* 1.1.

Glendenning, F. and Pearson, M. (1988), *The Black and Ethnic Minority Elder in Britain: Health Needs and Access to Services,* Working Papers on the Health of Older People, 6, Health Education Authority and University of Keele.

Golant, S.M. (1984), *A Place to Grow Old: the Meaning of Environment in Old Age,* New York: Columbia University Press.

Goldberg, E.M. (1983), 'Social care for the elderly: some issues for policy and practice', *Policy Studies,* 4.1, pp. 65-80.

Gooch, L.A. and Luxton, D.E.A. (1977), 'A new geriatric day hospital', *Nursing Mirror,* 145, pp. 36-38.

Gordon, C. (1988), 'The myth of family care? The elderly in the early 1930s', *Ageing and Society,* 8, pp. 287-320.

Greenfield, J.G. (1974), 'A departmental view', *Gerontologia Clinica,* 16, pp. 307-314.

Griffiths, Sir Roy (1988), *Community Care: Agenda for Action,* London: HMSO.

Hagestad, G. (1981), 'Problems and promises in the social psychology of interpersonal relations', in *Aging: Stability and Change in the Family,* (Eds. R.W. Fogel, et al), New York: Academic Press.

Hall, D. and Bytheway, B. (1980), 'The blocked bed: defining the problem', in *Transitions in Middle and Later Life,* (Ed. M.L. Johnson), British Society of Gerontology.

Hall, M. (1988), 'Geriatric Medicine Today', in *The Ageing Population - Burden or Challenge?,* (Eds. N. Wells and C. Freer), Basingstoke: Macmillan Press.

Hampshire County Council (1986), *Specialised Accommodation for the Elderly in Hampshire,* Winchester: Hampshire County Council.

Hannay, D.R. (1979), *The Symptom Iceberg: a Study of Community Health,* London: Routledge and Kegan Paul.

Harris, C.C. (1975), 'The social process of ageing', Ph.D. thesis, University of Wales.

Harris, C.C. (1987), *Redundancy and Recession,* Oxford: Blackwell.

Hazan, H. (1980), *The Limbo People - A Study of the Constitution of the Time Universe among the Aged,* London: Routledge and Kegan Paul.

Heidegger, M. (1962), *Being and Time,* New York: Harper and Row.

Henwood, M. and Wicks, M. (1984), *The Forgotten Army - Family Care and Elderly People,* London: Family Policy Study Centre.

Heron, A. (1961), *Preparation for Retirement: Solving New Problems,* London: National Council of Social Service.

Hildick-Smith, M. (1977), 'A study of day hospitals', Unpublished thesis, University of Cambridge.

Hildick-Smith, M. (1981), 'G.P.'s views of a geriatric day hospital', *Practitioner,* 225, pp. 127-131.

Hill, R. (1970), *Family Development in Three Generations,* Cambridge, Massachusetts: Schenkman.

Hinton, C. (1987), *Using Your Home as Capital,* Mitcham: Age Concern.

Holmgaard, B. with Pedersen, K.M. (1985), *Retirement: A Time for Transition: Denmark,* Dublin: European Foundation for Living and Working Conditions.

Horobin, G.W. (1987), Editorial, in *Why Day Care?,* Research Highlights in Social Work 14, London: Jessica Kingsley Publishers.

Horrocks, P. (1982), 'The case for geriatric medicine as an age-related specialty', in *Recent Advances in Geriatric Medicine,* Vol II, (Ed. B. Isaacs), pp. 260-7.

Housebuilders Federation (1988), 'Sheltered housing for sale - an advice note', 2nd edition, London: HBF.

Housebuilders Federation (1989), 'A guidance note - management and services', London: HBF.

Housebuilder Supplement (1988), 'Sheltered housing - a growing marketplace', *Housebuilder,* June.

Howell, S.C. (1983), 'The meaning of place in old age', in *Ageing and Milieu,* (Eds. G.D. Rowles and R.J. Ohta), New York: Academic Press.

Hudson, A. (1985), 'Feminism and social work: resistance or dialogue', *British Journal of Social Work,* 15, pp. 635-655.

Hunter, D.J. (1988), 'Community care: reacting to Griffiths', *King's Fund Briefing,* 1, London.

Irvine, R.E. (1980), 'Geriatric day hospitals - present trends', *Health Trends,* 3(12), pp. 68-71.

Itzin, C. (1984), 'The double jeopardy of ageism and sexism', in *Gerontology: Social and Behavioural Perspectives,* (Ed. D. Bromley), London: Croom Helm.

Johnson, M. (1978), 'That was your life: a biographical approach to later life', in *An Ageing Population*, (Eds. V. Carver and P. Liddiard), London: Hodder and Stoughton.

Johnson, P., Conrad, C. and Thomson, D. (1989), *Workers Versus Pensioners*, Centre for Economic Policy Research, Manchester: Manchester University Press.

Kalish, R. (1966), 'A continuum of subjectively perceived death', *The Gerontologist*, 6, pp. 72-77.

Kautzer, K. (1988), 'Empowering nursing home residents: a case study of "Living is for the Elderly", an activist nursing home organization', in *Qualitative Gerontology*, (Eds. S. Reinharz and G.D. Rowles), New York: Springer.

Kitwood, T. (1988), 'The contribution of psychology to the understanding of senile dementia ', in *Mental Health Problems in Old Age*, (Eds. B. Gearing, M. Johnson and T. Heller), Chichester: John Wiley.

Knapp, M.R.J. and Baines, B. (1987), 'Hidden cost multipliers for residential child care', *Local Government Studies*, 13.4, pp. 53-73.

Knapp, M.R.J., Bryson, D. and Lewis, J. (1984), 'The comprehensive costing of child care: the Suffolk cohort study', Discussion paper 355, PSSRU, University of Kent at Canterbury.

Laczko, F., Dale, A., Arber, S. and Gilbert, G.N. (1988), 'Early retirement in a period of high unemployment', *Journal of Social Policy*, 17.3, pp. 313-333.

Laczko, F. (1989), 'Between work and retirement: becoming "old" in the 1980s', in *Becoming and Being Old*, (Eds. B. Bytheway, T. Keil, P. Allatt and A. Bryman), London: SAGE.

Lakoff, G. and Johnson, M. (1980), *Metaphors We Live By*, Chicago: University of Chicago Press.

Lansley, J. and Pearson, M. (forthcoming), *Preparation for Retirement in the Member States of the European Community*, EC Commission, Directorate General V, Brussels.

Laslett, P. (1977), *Family Life and Illicit Love in Earlier Generations*, Cambridge: Cambridge University Press.

Leather, P. (1990), 'The potential and implications of home equity release in old age', *Housing Studies*, 5.1, pp. 3-13.

Leonard, D. (1980), *Sex and Generation*, London: Tavistock.

Lieberman, M.A. and Tobin S.S. (1983), *The Experience of Old Age*, New York: Basic Books.

Lipman, A.R. and Slater, R. (1975), *Architectural Design Implications of Residential Homes for Old People*, Final Report, Social Science Research Council.

Lipman, A.R. and Slater, R. (1977), 'Homes for old people: toward a positive environment', *The Gerontologist*, 17.2, pp. 146-56.

Llewellyn Smith, H. (Ed.) (1930-34), *New Survey of London Life and Labour*, 10v, London: King.

London Borough of Wandsworth (1979), *Staffing and Dependency*, Social Services Department.

Lurie, E.E. and Swan, J.H. (1987), *Serving the Mentally Ill Elderly*, New York: Lexington Books.

Majone, G. (1976), 'Standard-setting and the theory of institutional choice', *Policy and Politics*, 4.2, pp. 35-52.

Marshall, M. (1983), *Social Work with Old People*, London: Macmillan.

Matthews, S. (1979), *The Social World of Old Women: Management of Self Identity*, Beverly Hills: Sage.

McCoy, P. (1983), 'Short-term residential care for elderly people - an answer to growing older', in *Ageing in Modern Society*, (Ed. D. Jerrome), London: Croom Helm.

McGoldrick, A.E. and Cooper, C.L. (1988), *Early Retirement*, Aldershot: Gower Press.

McKee, L. (1987), 'Households during unemployment', in *Give and Take in Families*, (Eds. J. Brannen and G. Wilson), London: Allen and Unwin.

McLeod, E. (1987), 'Some lessons in teaching feminist social work', *Issues in Social Work Education*, 7.1, pp. 29-36.

Meacher, M. (1972), *Taken for a Ride*, London: Longman.

Millard, P. (1988), 'New horizons in hospital based care', in *The Ageing Population - Burden or Challenge?*, (Eds. N. Wells and C. Freer), Basingstoke: Macmillan Press.

Miller, S.J. (1965), 'The social dilemma of the aging leisure participant', in *Older People and their Social World*, (Eds. A.M. Rose, and W.A. Peterson), Philadephia: F.A. Davis.

Ministry of Health (1957), *Geriatric Services and the Care of the Chronic Sick*, London: HMSO.

Moller, I.H. (1987), 'Early retirement in Denmark', *Ageing and Society*, 7.4, pp. 427-443.

Morgan, D.L. (1983), 'Failing health and the desire for independence: two conflicting aspects of health care in old age', *Social Problems*, 30.1, pp. 40-50.

Morley, D. (1974), 'Day care and leisure provision for the elderly', *Age Concern Today*.

Muir-Gray, J.A. (1984), 'The prevention of family breakdown', *Nursing Mirror*, 158(23), pp. 16-17.

Muir-Gray, J.A. (1988), 'Living environments for the elderly - living at home', in *The Ageing Population - Burden or Challenge?*, (Eds. N. Wells and C. Freer), Basingstoke: Macmillan Press.

Murdock, A. (1986), 'Confusional states in elderly persons' homes residents: a process of label acquisition', in *Dependency and Interdependency in Old Age: Theoretical Perspectives and Policy Alternatives*, (Eds. C. Phillipson, M. Bernard and P. Strang), London: Croom Helm.

Murphy, E.W. (1985), 'Day care - who and what is it for?', *New Age*, 31, pp. 6-9.

National Federation of Housing Associations (1985), 'Housing association partnerships with private developers - leasehold sheltered housing', London: NFHA.

National Federation of Housing Associations (1988), 'Leasehold schemes for the elderly - ten years on: a review', London: NFHA.

Natsoulas, T. (1983), 'Concepts of consciousness', *Journal of Mind and Behaviour*, 4.1, pp. 13-59.

Nissel, M. and Bonnerjea, L. (1982), *Family Care of the Handicapped Elderly: Who Pays?*, London: Policy Studies Institute.

Nolan, M.R. (1986), 'Day care in perspective - a comparative study of two day hospitals for the elderly', Unpublished M.A. Thesis, University of Wales.

Oakley, A. (1981), 'Interviewing women', in *Doing Feminist Research*, (Ed. H. Roberts), London: Routledge and Kegan Paul.

Office of Population, Censuses and Surveys (1982), *General Household Survey, 1980*, London: HMSO.

Office of Population, Censuses and Surveys, (1987), *Hospital In-patient Enquiry 1985: Summary tables*, London: HMSO.

Parker, G. (1985), 'With due care and attention - a review of research on informal care', Occasional Paper no. 2, London: Family Policy Studies Centre.

Peace, S., Kellaher L. and Willcocks D. (1983), *The Essence of Home*, Seminar report, Centre on Environment for the Handicapped.

Peace, S. (1986), 'The forgotten female: an analysis of the effects of social policy on the lives of older women', in *Ageing and Social Policy*, (Eds. C. Phillipson and A. Walker), Aldershot: Gower Press.

Pearson, M., Pick, K. and Lansley, J. (forthcoming), *Preparation for Retirement in Europe: Practices and Perspectives*, EC Commission, Directorate General V, Brussels.

Phillips, M. (1988), 'Public faces in private places', *Social Services Insight*, February, pp. 10-12.

Phillipson, C. (1981), 'Women in later life: patterns of control and subordination', in *Controlling Women: the Normal and the Deviant*, (Eds. B. Hutter and G. Williams), London: Croom Helm.

Phillipson, C. (1982) *Capitalism and the Construction of Old Age*, Basingstoke: Macmillan Press.

Phillipson, C. and Strang, P. (1983), 'The impact of pre-retirement education: a longitudinal evaluation', Department of Adult Education, University of Keele.

Potter, P. and Wiseman, V. (1989), *Improving Residential Practice: Promoting Choice in Homes for Elderly People*, London: National Institute of Social Work.

Qureshi, H. and Simons, K. (1987), 'Resources within families: caring for elderly people', in *Given and Take in Families*, (Eds. J. Brannen and G. Wilson), London: Allen and Unwin.

Rapoport, A. (1982), *The Meaning of the Built Environment*, London: Sage.

Richards, M. (1987), 'Developing the content of practice teaching', *Social Work Education*, 6.2, pp. 4-9.

Rideout, E. (1986), 'Hope, morale and adaptation in patients with chronic heart disease', *Journal of Advanced Nursing*, 11, pp. 429-438.

Ritcey, S. (1982), 'Substituting an interactionalist for a normative model in research', *Resources in Feminist Research*, 2, pp. 220-221.

Rodwell, G. (1985), 'Urizen and social work education: a comment on 'Reflection on the life of a group in a geriatric hospital' by Margaret Valk', *Issues in Social Work Education*, 5.1, pp. 67-69.

Rosser, K.C. and Harris C.C. (1965), *The Family and Social Change*, London: Routledge and Kegan Paul.

Rowles, G.D. (1978), *Prisoners of Space*, Boulder, Colorado: Westview Press.

Rowles, G.D. (1981), 'The surveillance zone as meaningful space for the aged', *The Gerontologist*, 21.3, pp. 304-311.

Rowles, G.D. (1983), 'Geographical dimensions of social support in rural Appalachia', in *Ageing and Milieu*, (Eds. G.D. Rowles and R.J. Ohta), New York: Academic Press.

Rowlings, C. (1981), *Social Work with Elderly People*, London: George Allen and Unwin.

Rubin, S.G. and Davies, G.M. (1975), 'Bed blocking by elderly patients in general hospital wards', *Age and Ageing*, 4, pp. 142-147.

Sager, A. and Sterling, H. (1982), 'Mobilizing and coordinating increased informal long-term care', Levinson Policy Institute, Brandeis University, Waltham, Massachusetts.

Sahlins, M. (1965), 'On the sociology of primitive exchange', in *The Relevance of Models in Social Anthropology*, (Ed. M. Banton), London: Tavistock.

Salaman, E. (1970), *A Collection of Moments: A Study of Involuntary Memories*, London: Longmans.

Scheffer, W. (1981-82), 'Retirement in Prospect (PiZ) and women', *Adult Education and Retirement*, European Bureau of Adult Education Newsletter, pp. 26-27.

Schultz, C.E. (1974), 'The public use of the private interest', Brookings Institute, Washington D.C.

Scott-Whyte, S. (1985), *Supplementary Benefits and Residential Care*, Report of a Joint Central and Local Government Working Party, London: Department of Health and Social Security.

Seymour, D.G. and Pringle, R. (1982), 'Elderly patients in a general surgical unit: do they block beds?', *British Medical Journal*, 284, pp. 1921-1923.

Shanas, E., Townsend, P., Wedderburn, D., Friis, H., Milhoj, P. and Stehower, J. (1968), *Old People in Three Industrial Societies*, London: Routledge and Kegan Paul.

Shortland, S. (1985), 'Pre-retirement counseling in practice', *Personnel Executive*, January, pp. 29-32.

Sinclair, I., Stanforth, L. and O'Connor, P. (1988), 'Factors predicting admission of elderly people to Local Authority residential care', *British Journal of Social Work*, 18.3, pp. 251-68.

Sixsmith, A.J. (1986a), 'Independence and home in later life', in *Dependency and Interdependency in Old Age: Theoretical Perspectives and Policy Alternatives*, (Eds. C. Phillipson, M. Bernard and P. Strang), London: Croom Helm.

Sixsmith, A.J. (1986b), 'The meaning of home: an exploratory study of environmental experience', *Journal of Environmental Psychology*, 6, pp. 281-298.

Sixsmith, A.J. (1988), 'Remembering-in-the-world: an experiential analysis of the relationship between memories and the home', Paper presented to the IAPS-10 conference, Delft University, July 5-8.

Smith, G. and Cantley, C. (1983), 'Day care made simple', *Health and Social Services Journal*, 93, pp. 692-693.

Stanley, L. and Wise, S. (1979), 'Feminist research, feminist consciousness and the experience of sexism', *Womens Studies International Quarterly*, 2, pp. 259-279.

Starr, J. (1983), 'Toward a social phenomenology of ageing: studying the self process in biographical work', *International Journal of Ageing and Human Development*, 16.4, pp. 255-270.

Stevenson, O. and Parsloe, P. (1978), *Social Service Teams: a Practitioners' View*, London: HMSO.

Sussman, M.B. (1965), 'Relationships of adult children with their parents in the United States', in *Social Structure and the Family: Generational Relations*, (Eds. E. Shanas and G.F. Streib), New Jersey: Prentice Hall.

Sutherland, C. (1986), 'Feminist research: a voice of our own', in *Gender Reclaimed: Women in Social Work*, (Eds. H. Marchant and B. Waring), Sydney NSW: Hale and Iremonger.

Swank, C. (1982), *Phased Retirement: the European Experience*, National Council for Alternative Work Patterns, Washington D.C.

Swank, C. (1983), 'Retiring in phases: the European corporate experience', *Transatlantic Perspectives*, 9, August, pp. 9-11.

Szinovacz, M. (1982), 'Introduction: research on women's retirement', in *Women's Retirement: Policy Implications of Recent Research*, (Ed. M. Szinovacz), Beverly Hills: Sage.

Taylor, H. (1987), *Growing Older Together - Elderly Owner Occupiers and their Housing*, London: Centre for Policy on Ageing.

Technical Working Group (1987), Report to the Secretary, Technical working group on private financing of longterm care for the elderly, Washington, D.C.

Thompson, M.K. (1974), 'A general practitioner looks at day care', *Gerontologia Clinica*, 16(5-6), pp. 258-262.

Thomson, D. (1986), 'Welfare and the historians', in *The World We Have Gained*, (Eds. L. Bonfield, et al), Oxford: Blackwell.

Tibbett, J.E. (1987), 'Day care - a good thing?', in *Why Day Care?*, Research Highlights in Social Work 14, (Ed. G.W. Horobin), London: Jessica Kingsley Publishers.

Tinker, A. (1977), 'What sort of housing do the elderly want?' *Housing Review*, May/June, pp. 54-55.

Tinker, A. (1984), *Staying at Home: Helping Elderly People*, London: HMSO.

Townsend, P. (1962), *The Last Refuge*, London: Routledge and Kegan Paul.

Townsend, P. (1963), *The Family Life of Old People*, Harmondsworth: Penguin.

Townsend, P. (1986), 'Ageing and social policy' in *Ageing and Social Policy - a Critical Assessment*, (Eds. C. Phillipson, and A. Walker), Aldershot: Gower Press.

Tyndall, R.M. (1978), 'Day hospital dilemma - when patients refuse', *Modern Geriatrics*, 8.2, pp. 34-37.

Ungerson, C. (1987), *Policy is Personal*, London: Tavistock.

Valk, M. (1985), 'Reflections on the life of a group in a geriatric hospital', *Issue in Social Work Education*, 5.1, pp. 13-23.

Victor, C.R. and Vetter, N.J. (1985), 'A one-year follow-up of patients discharged from geriatrics and general medical units in Wales', *Archive of Gerontology and Geriatrics*, 4, pp. 117-24.

Wadsworth, M.E.J., Sinclair, S. and Wirz, H.M. (1972), 'A geriatric day hospital and its system of care', *Social Science and Medicine*, 6.4, pp. 507-525.

Wagner Committee (1988), *Residential Care: A Positive Choice*, Report of the Independent Review of Residential Care, London: HMSO.

Wagstaff, S. (1979), 'On to care - a study of a Burslem day centre', Unpublished M.A. thesis, University of Keele.

Walker, R. and Hardman, G. (1988), 'The financial resources of the elderly or paying your own way in old age', in *Social Security and Community Care*, (Eds. S. Baldwin, G. Parker and R. Walker), Aldershot: Gower Press, pp. 45-73.

Wall, R. (1989), 'The living arrangements of the elderly in Europe in the 1980s', in *Becoming and Being Old*, (Eds. B. Bytheway, T. Keil, P. Allatt and A. Bryman), London: SAGE.

Wall, R., Schurer, K. and Laslett, P. (1988), 'The changing form of the English household 1891-1921: a four community study', mimeo paper.

Ward, R.A. (1979), *The Ageing Experience*, New York: Lippincott.

Weers, A. (1980), 'Centres de formation et marche de la preparation a la retraite', *Cahiers du CEPES*, 15, October, Grenoble.

Welsh Office (1985), *A Good Old Age - An Initiative on the Care of the Elderly in Wales*, Cardiff: Welsh Office.

West Sussex County Council (1986), 'Rest homes, nursing homes and private sheltered housing in West Sussex', Lewes: West Sussex CC.

Wheeler, R. (1985), *Don't Move: We've Got You Covered*, London: Institute of Housing.

Whelan, B.J., O'Higgins, K. and Whelan, C.T. (1985), *Retirement; a Time of Transition: Ireland*, Dublin: European Foundation for Living and Working Conditions.

Wiener, C. (1978), 'The burden of rheumatoid arthritis: tolerating the uncertainty', in *An Ageing Population*, (Eds. V. Carver and P. Liddiard), London: Hodder and Stoughton.

Wilkin, D. (1986), 'Theoretical and conceptual issues in the measurement of dependency', Centre for Primary Care Research, University of Manchester.

Wilkin, D. and Hughes, B. (1986), 'The elderly and the health services', in *Ageing and Social Policy - a Critical Assessment*, (Eds. C. Phillipson and A. Walker), Aldershot: Gower Press.

Willcocks, D., Peace, S. and Kellaher, L. (1987), *Private Lives in Public Places: a Research-based Critique of Residential Life in Local Authority Old People's Homes*, London: Tavistock.

Williams, G. (1986), 'Meeting the housing needs of the elderly: private initiative or public responsibility?', OP 17, University of Manchester: Department of Planning and Landscape.

Williams, G. (1990a), 'Development niches and specialist housebuilders - an overview of private sheltered housing in Britain', *Housing Studies*, 5.1, pp. 14-23.

Williams, G. (1990b), *Housing in Retirement: Elderly Lifestyles and Private Initiative*, Aldershot: Avebury Press.

Williams, G. (1990c), 'Housing associations and the elderly: the role of leasehold initiatives', OP 23, University of Manchester: Department of Planning and Landscape.

Williams, R.G.A. (1980), 'Innovations in community care - a study of interpretations in a day hospital', *Social Science and Medicine*, 149, pp. 501-510.

Wise, S. (1985), 'Becoming a feminist social worker', *Manchester Studies in Sexual Politics*, 6.

Wittgenstein, L. (1958), *Philosophical Investigations*, Oxford: Blackwell.

Woodford-Williams, E. and Alvarez, A.S. (1964), 'Four years experience of a day hospital in geriatric practice', *Gerontologia Clinica*, 7 (2-3), pp. 86-106.

Wright, M. (1984), 'Using the past to help the present', *Community Care*, October 11th, pp. 20-22.

Contributors

Miriam Bernard, Centre for Social Gerontology, University of Keele.

Bill Bytheway, Department of Epidemiology and Community Medicine, University of Wales College of Medicine, Cardiff, and University College of Swansea.

Oliver Coles, Social Services Department, Durham County Council.

Bleddyn Davies, Personal Social Services Research Unit, University of Kent at Canterbury.

Jane Falkingham, Department of Economic History, and Welfare State Programme, London School of Economics.

Chris Gordon, The Netherland Interuniversity Demographic Institute, Den Haag, The Netherlands.

Vera Ivers, Beth Johnson Foundation, Stoke-on-Trent.

Julia Johnson, Centre for Applied Social Studies, University College of Swansea.

John Lansley, Department of Sociology and Institute of Human Ageing, University of Liverpool.

Pat Le Riche, Department of Applied Social Studies, Goldsmiths' College, University of London.

Jackie Lucas, Department of Sociology and Anthropology, University College of Swansea.

Michael Nolan, Centre for Social Policy Research and Development, University College of North Wales, Bangor.

Maggie Pearson, Department of General Practice and Institute of Human Ageing, University of Liverpool.

Judith Phillips, School of Economic and Social Studies, University of East Anglia.

Kathy Pick, Institute of Human Ageing, University of Liverpool.

Chloe Rowlings, Specialist Social Worker, Social Services Department, London.

Andrew Sixsmith, Department of Psychiatry and Institute of Human Ageing, University of Liverpool.

Christina Victor, Community Medicine and Nursing Research Unit, St. Mary's Hospital, London.

Gwyn Williams, Department of Planning and Landscape, University of Manchester.